THE CLASSIC

KONKAN COOKBOOK

THE CLASSIC
KONKAN
COOKBOOK

Jyotsna Shahane

Based on the Original Recipes of
Narayani Nayak

HarperCollins *Publishers* India

First published in India by
HarperCollins Publishers in 2020
A-75, Sector 57, Noida, Uttar Pradesh 201301, India
www.harpercollins.co.in

Copyright © Jyotsna Shahane 2020

P-ISBN 978-93-5357-406-2
E-ISBN 978-93-5357-441-3

Designed by HarperCollins Publishers India
Printed and bound at Thomson Press (India) Ltd
Photography Jyotsna Shahane

For Ravi, Namita and Devika,
who have discovered the joy of cooking
and the secret ingredient in all good food.

Contents

*Baby Potatoes in an Onion &
Tomato Gravy*

500
Easy Recipes

Narayani V. Nayak

a new approach

Introduction

◆◆◆

When Narayani Nayak brought out her book, *Cookery Craft* (see photo, left), in 1952, very few cookbooks were available in India. Most housewives gleaned information from handwritten notes passed down from mother to daughter. Some books were written by Britishers stationed in India, giving Anglo-Indian recipes for Cofta ka Carree, Quorema's, Country Captain, Doopiajas, Hindustanee and Hussenee curries recorded from conversations with their khansamas, among several more pages of household and housekeeping tips and advice.

It was only in the late 1950s that women's magazines started being published, and soon recipes printed in them were prized, cut out and preserved.

When *Cookery Craft* received such 'a good reception from the public', Nayak resolved to revise and rewrite it 'to serve as a convenient kitchen companion to every housewife, who is receptive to new ideas and is interested in good cooking, and particularly to the new bride about to start her own home'.

In 1964, she published *500 Easy Recipes* that incorporated her two earlier books (*Cookery Craft* and *200 Recipes*). This book was extremely popular among Konkani-speaking people in India, predating all other Konkani cookbooks by a good 15 years.

What makes the book stand out, even today, is Nayak's ability to give exact weights and measures. Up until then, cookbooks were quite vague about amounts, mentioning only ingredients and a technique of cooking that was not always logical or easy to follow.

In Konkani food, unlike other cuisines in India, each preparation is named according to the ingredients used and the degree of density. Nayak followed a cogent method, which she detailed in each recipe, and gave an indication of the consistency of each preparation (thick, solid, soupy, gravy, etc.).

To think that Nayak was educated only up to Class 5 is amazing. She was born in Karkala in Udupi district and learnt to write only after her marriage. She also taught herself English, among other languages, for the sake of her children.

Her grandson recalls her carrying her 'quaint notebooks everywhere, recording each and everything when in the kitchen. When the pages of many such notebooks were filled, her husband encouraged her to publish them'. These became *Cookery Craft* and, later, *500 Easy Recipes*. She calls 'the countless hours spent ... first and last a labour of love'.

The book was a huge success and was reprinted in 1965, 1966, 1979 and 1986 before it went out of print.

It did, indeed, become the go-to book for Konkani brides, in much the same way as *The Joy of Cooking* by Irma Rombauer or *Mastering the Art of French Cooking* by Julia Child, Louisette Bertholle and Simone Beck was for brides in the US. One of my friends, Jyoti Prabhu, recalls leaving Indian shores to join her doctor husband as a newly-married woman of 19. Her suitcase was full of her trousseau of glittering sarees, jewellery, slippers and this cookbook. 'The sarees and jewellery were all put away in a cupboard, hardly ever to be used again, but the cookbook was utilized every single day, till I knew it all by heart. It fell apart when I photocopied it for the sixth time, for my daughter.'

My own introduction to authentic Konkani food was at the table of Nalini Karnad in Bombay in the 1970s. The lunch-time meal was created by her 99-year-old mother and herself, with ingredients bought fresh every day from the neighbourhood vegetable market.

Every meal, for me, was a journey of discovery. Of ingredients unknown, of exotic tastes and surprising textures. The lunch thali was dotted with all kinds of vegetarian preparations. Two types of lentils, four vegetables, chutneys, pickles, salads, rice, rotis, buttermilk and homemade curds were part of a daily meal.

Part of the charm was to be involved in the conversation between four generations of the family seated at the table. It was always witty, informed, thoroughly opinionated, humorous and eclectic in the choice of subject.

Forty-odd years of sharing such meals have given me a fondness for the taste of Konkani food, a liking that led me to learn and reproduce the preparations at my own table for my family and in my blog on Indian food, The Cooks Cottage, which I began writing in 2004.

A few characteristics that struck me were the freshness and simplicity of the food. Then there was the use of all kinds of vegetables, some quite unknown to me at the time. Lastly, the fact that nothing was wasted. Every part of vegetable or fruit was used. Stalks, leaves, and peels were used to great effect in curries, chutneys, and pickles. In a country where many people do not have enough to eat, this resonated with me.

When Nayak wrote the book, the average housewife in India spent almost the whole day in the kitchen, cooking food from morning to night, for her husband and family. With an average of four to six children per household, large amounts were cooked. The day began with a cooked breakfast, carried on to a hot lunch and ended with a large dinner, interspersed with helpings of snacks and sweets as well. A meal, served on a thali or banana leaf, consisted of a couple of vegetables, a lentil dish, a fried snack, two chutneys and a salad besides a sweet dish and buttermilk to wash it all down.

Ways of cooking and eating have changed today. Most people can find time to cook just one or two main dishes and these must provide all the nutrients necessary for healthy living. Besides changing from the old measures of tola and seers to grams and cups, I have rewritten most of the recipes to increase or decrease the amount where necessary, suggested substitutions if the main ingredient is not easily available, shortened the preparation time by using modern appliances, and given alternatives to those who do not have the time or energy to start from scratch.

The recipes were tested by me over a period of two years and then retested by my many Konkani friends, who gave insights into spicing and traditions and names in each corner of the region. Some were rigorously tested by friends from the US, who were totally new to the cuisine, to check for ease of use, clarity, method and measures. One was vastly overqualified for the job, being an auditor of NASA reports.

The addition of red and green chillies in most recipes has been reduced as many recipes were overpoweringly pungent. They can, in fact, be made optional, so the flavour of the main ingredient comes through. I have added more popular meat and seafood recipes from the region as the original book had very few, surprisingly so, since seafood is available in abundance on the Konkan coast.

All these changes have been made with a view to making this cuisine more accessible and reproducible by interested cooks around the world.

As with the original book, this has been a labour of love.

The Roots of Konkani Cuisine

Nayak's book is notable because the recipes are not particular to any caste or religion; they span the cuisine of the entire Konkani-speaking community.

The Konkan is a narrow coastal plain, barely 50 kilometres wide, a belt of land that stretches from Maharashtra in the north where Thane, Raigad, Ratnagiri and Sindhudurg form part of the region, through Goa and Uttara Kannada (North Canara) from Karwar though Ankola to Honawar to Dakshin Kannada (South Canara) including Dharwar and Mangalore. It is bounded on the east by the Sahyadri Range (the Western Ghats) and on the west by the Arabian Sea.

The Konkani language is spoken in all these places as well as in north Kerala, in Kasaragod, and even further south to Kochi and Trivandrum.

Since the entire region faces the windward side of the Western Ghats, it receives very heavy rainfall in the monsoon but faces paucity of water during the summer months so that only certain crops do well on a larger scale.

The climatic conditions have sustained a rich diversity of flora with a high level of rare and indigenous plant species. This is a characteristic of the Konkan region that continues to fascinate people, from early explorers and adventurers, such as Jan Huyghen van Linschoten. Besides mapping navigational routes to the East Indies, Linschoten drew detailed pictures of the exotic and abundant flora and fauna he encountered in the Konkan region during his travels in 1583 when he was appointed secretary to the Archbishop of Goa, Dominican Vicente da Fonseca.

Even now, the Konkan sustains strange and exotic plants not seen in other parts of India. The region is known for crops such as coconut, rice, finger millet, cashewnut, kokum, mango, areca nut, jackfruit and pulses. Vegetables grow in abundance in kitchen gardens, with little encouragement in the form of fertilizers or pesticides. A host of gourds, greens and tubers proliferate among the lush undergrowth of the area.

Konkani cuisine is defined by these crops, easily available in the entire coastal region. Coconuts form an integral part of almost every dish, with pulses, greens, cashewnuts and fruits adding nutrition, texture and taste rarely encountered in other regional cuisines of India. Black pepper, Szechuan pepper and red chillies, again commonly grown in this area, pep up almost every dish, vegetarian and non-vegetarian.

Some of the more unusual ingredients used in the cuisine are jackfruit, wood apple, mango ginger, colocasia tubers and leaves, wild potato, breadfruit, banana pith and flowers, drumsticks and their flowers, and pumpkin flowers.

Souring agents like tamarind, bilimbi, mango pith, and kokum are regularly used to balance the bitterness or pungency left by some ingredients in the dish.

Spices like fenugreek and asafoetida are combined with the more common mustard seed and red chilli to add flavour.

The botanic/scientific, common, local, and vernacular names of all these fruits, vegetables, flowers and spices can be found in the glossary (page 179).

Konkani Cooking Terms

Ambat is a bland preparation using coconut masala as its basic ingredient. It is seasoned either with onions or with mustard (rai). It is fairly thick in consistency.

Ghushi is like ambat but not as bland.

Koddel is a curry slightly hotter than ghushi. It is seasoned with mustard (rai) and asafoetida (hing), or with garlic.

Bendhi is a very pungent curry with coconut lesser in quantity than what is used in the above three. Seasoning is as for koddel.

Humman is a curry with a gravy made with or without coconut.

Sukke is an almost solid and dry curry with coconut masala to which coriander seeds and urad (black gram) dal are usually added.

Bhuthy is like sukke but the masala contains ginger, and onions are used for seasoning.

Khathkhatho is a thick curry which is not seasoned. A dessert spoon of oil is added to the finished curry.

Sagle is also a thick curry with coconut masala, using methi and coriander seeds as basic ingredients. Vegetables used in this are either cut into big pieces or used in their entirety.

Saasam is of the same consistency as sagle. The coconut masala in this contains a little raw mustard.

Hasi is a vegetable salad where the vegetables and masala are used unboiled. Hasi in Kannada means raw.

Koot is like hasi but with the exception that the vegetables are fried and added.

Thambli is an uncooked preparation containing masala.

Kadi is a preparation with coconut masala and is thinner than thambli but thicker than saar.

Saar is a thin, watery preparation with coconut masala. Thambli, kadi and saar are coconut gravies without any vegetables in them.

Chutney is a dry, uncooked, thick preparation with coconut as a main ingredient.

Bharth is a semi-solid preparation using uncooked masala mixed with cooked and mashed vegetables.

Gozzu and **Bajji** are identical preparations. The ingredients of the former are not mashed as thoroughly as of the latter.

Upkari is a simple preparation of seasoned and cooked vegetables.

Saarupkari is same as upkari but the vegetables and grams are cooked with an extra amount of water so that there is a little gravy in the finished preparation. One makes a saar and the thick gram leftover is made into an upkari.

Curry is a general term used for preparations which are a little more elaborate than the ordinary upkari.

Dalithoi is dal water (thoya is a Sanskrit word, meaning water).

Sambar is a liquid curry fairly thick in consistency with vegetables and dal as the basic ingredients.

Kolambu is a liquid curry like sambar, with vegetables in it. Dal is omitted.

Morkolambu is like kolambu and sambar with buttermilk and a little coconut masala added to it. Mor is a Tamil word for buttermilk.

Kootu is a thick curry with dal and vegetables as the basic ingredients and with a little coconut masala added to it.

Thambli is a non-greasy, non-spicy, cooling curry generally served with a Bendhi, which is hot and spicy, it balances the meal.

Basic Recipes

•••

EXTRACTING COCONUT MILK

Husk a coconut, pierce a hole in the soft eye on top of the shell and empty out the water. Crack the shell by putting the coconut in a plastic bag and hitting it with a pestle. Prise the flesh off the shell with a blunt knife and chop into pieces.

Put the pieces into a blender and grind till fine. Add 150 ml (1 cup) of water and blend again. (Use warm water in cold weather.) Pass this mixture through a strainer or a fine muslin cloth. This is the first pressing and gives you thick coconut milk. Repeat the process with another 300 ml water for thin coconut milk. Keep refrigerated till ready to use.

Note: Reduce the amount of water added as per the quantity of coconut used.

SPROUTING GRAM

Wash and soak 250 g (2 cups) of gram in 6 cups of water. Keep covered for 8–10 hours, or overnight. The next morning, drain the water completely. Use a clean cloth to bundle and tie up the gram, or keep covered in a warm place for a day. By evening, the gram will have sprouted. Soak the sprouted gram for another 8 hours to loosen the skin. Remove the skin, if preferred, before cooking.

Retain the skin of masoor (split red) dal, kulith (horse gram) and tuvar (pigeon pea) dal as it does not peel off despite soaking.

ROASTING SPICES

Take a non-stick frying pan, a tava or a vagharia (tadka pan) depending on the amount of spices you need to roast.

Heat over a medium fire, then turn to low as you put the spices in the pan. It is best to do each spice separately as they burn easily, which will result in a bitter taste. When light brown or when the spice gives off a faint fragrance, remove from the pan and let it cool before grinding.

Break red chillies into bits before roasting. Smear a little oil on the chillies and mix with a pinch of salt before roasting. This prevents the chillies from giving off a pungent odour.

ROASTING GRATED COCONUT

If you don't have a coconut scraper, grate coconut pieces on a fine grater.

Heat a non-stick frying pan over a low flame to roast the grated coconut. Spread it out evenly across the base of the pan, stirring frequently so that it browns evenly. It takes a fair amount of time to get it just the right colour which is a deep golden brown. Do not burn.

When it has become crisp and a little oil coats the bottom of the pan, the coconut is ready to use.

PULPING TAMARIND

Soak 1-inch ball of tamarind (imli) in two tablespoons of water for 15 minutes. Using your fingertips, loosen the flesh of the tamarind. Strain through a tea strainer or a piece of muslin to make a thin paste.

PREPPING

Karela (bitter gourd) and sooran (yams)

To reduce the bitterness of karela, kakora (teasel gourd) and drumstick, soak the cut pieces in buttermilk for 4 hours prior to use. Add a pinch of turmeric to the buttermilk.

Sooran (elephant yam) and arvi (colocasia tubers) can sometimes irritate the throat. To prevent this, add a little tamarind juice while cooking. You can also rub the chopped vegetables with tamarind and salt, let it stand for a while, squeeze out and discard any accumulated water and then cook.

Saffron

Soak a pinch of saffron in ½ tsp water and then grind to a smooth paste.

Suji (wheat semolina)
Add a little ghee, salt or a few drops of lime juice to the suji to prevent the grains sticking together.

MAKING RICE
For long grain or basmati rice, wash a cup of rice 5 times till the water runs clear. Soak in 2 cups of water for 15 minutes. Drain the water.

Put the washed rice in a heavy-bottomed pan and cover with double the amount of water, in this case 2 cups. Bring to a boil, turn heat to low, cover with a tight-fitting lid and cook for 15 minutes. Do not open to check the rice.

When the 15 minutes are over, turn the heat off and resist the urge to uncover the pot and check the rice. Let it stand for 10 minutes.

Your rice is done ... perfectly.

TADKA - SEASONING YOUR DISH
To get the best results, heat oil to smoking point and then add the ingredients in the order noted. Generally, mustard seed (rai) is fried first and when it splutters and pops the remaining ingredients are added one by one.

HOW TO CORRECT TASTE
Add a tablespoon of milk or a teaspoon of jaggery or sugar to correct the taste in case of too much saltiness or sourness.

Curry
Powders

Garam Masala Powder 1

Makes 6 tablespoons

INGREDIENTS

Cumin seeds 1 tsp

Black cumin seeds 1 tsp

Black cardamom 1 tsp

Cinnamon, broken 2 tsp

Black peppercorns 2 tsp

Cloves 1 tsp

A pinch of nutmeg

Bay leaves, broken 2

METHOD

Dry roast each spice separately in a frying pan over a low fire, till light brown. When cool, put them in a grinder jar and powder till fine. Store the spice mix in a clean, dry jar.

Note: This masala can also be made without roasting the spices.

Used in: Masoor Dal with Potatoes (page 88).

Garam Masala Powder 2

Makes 150 g

INGREDIENTS

Coriander seeds 125 g

Dry red chillies 17 pieces

Turmeric ¾-inch long piece

Cinnamon, broken into bits
3 inches

Cloves 15 pieces

Peppercorns 1 tsp

Cumin seeds 1 tsp

Poppy seeds 1 tsp

Sesame seeds 2 tsp

Fenugreek seeds ½ tsp

METHOD

Dry roast each spice separately in a frying pan till light brown. Ensure that the spices do not burn or the masala mix will taste bitter. When cool, grind all the spices together into a powder and store in a clean, dry jar.

Used in: Prawn Pickle (page 165).

Huli Powder

Makes 70 g

INGREDIENTS

Coriander seeds 65 g

Small dry red chillies 22 pieces

Fenugreek seeds ¼ tsp

Vegetable oil ½ tbsp

METHOD

Heat the oil in a frying pan and fry each ingredient separately over a low flame till light brown. Stir continuously to brown evenly. Grind them together to make a powder and store in a clean, dry jar.

Variation: Add 1 tsp cumin seeds to the ingredients to make rasam powder.

Used in: Kook Upkari (page 51)

Coconut Curry Powder

Makes 60 g

INGREDIENTS

Half a medium-sized coconut, finely grated (or scraped)

Vegetable oil 1 tsp

Coriander seeds 1 tbsp

Dry red chillies 6

Turmeric powder ½ tsp

Tamarind ball ½ inch

METHOD

Heat a non-stick frying pan and roast the coconut over a low to medium heat, stirring continuously, till well browned. This takes time and should not be rushed or the coconut chars and becomes bitter. Heat a teaspoon of oil and fry the coriander seeds and red chillies separately. Add the turmeric powder to the hot spices and stir. Grind all the ingredients together till smooth. Keep in a clean, dry jar.

This curry powder will keep fresh for a month.

Mangalore Rasam Powder

Makes 120 g

INGREDIENTS

Coriander seeds 70 g

Dry red chillies 15 g

Chana dal (husked Bengal gram) 30 g

Fenugreek seeds ¼ tsp

A big pinch of turmeric powder

Cumin seeds ¼ tsp

Black peppercorns 6

METHOD

Roast all the spices separately in a frying pan over a low fire till light brown. Powder them together and store in a clean dry jar.

Used in this recipe: Rasam (page 89)

Mangalore Sambar Powder

Makes 75 g (about 12 heaped tablespoons)

INGREDIENTS

Dry red chillies 50 g

Oil 1 tsp

Salt ½ tsp

Moong dal 1 tbsp

Coriander seeds 15 g

Peppercorns 10

Cumin seeds 1/3 tsp

Fenugreek seeds ¼ tsp

Turmeric 1/3 tsp

Asafoetida (hing) powder ¼ tsp

METHOD

Put the chillies in a pan and pour the oil and sprinkle the salt over them. Mix well with a spoon. Roast slowly in a non-stick pan over a low heat. Remove the chillies and roast the other whole ingredients, separately, one by one, over low heat stirring constantly to prevent burning. Grind all together with the turmeric and asafoetida powder in a coffee grinder till fine. Cool and bottle in a clean, dry jar.

Used in: Mangalorean Sambar (page 83)

Salads

---◆◆◆---

Pumpkin Salad (Duddi Koshambari)

Serves 2-4

INGREDIENTS

Red pumpkin (kaddu), finely-chopped 150 g

Seasoning

Vegetable oil 1 tbsp

Mustard seeds ¼ tsp

Green chilli, slit, deseeded and julienned 1

Onion (medium-sized), chopped 1

Coconut milk 5 tbsp (page 18)

Vinegar 1 tbsp

Salt to taste

METHOD

- Steam the pumpkin pieces for about 10 minutes till cooked.
- Heat the oil and fry the mustard seeds, green chillies and onions. As soon as the onions are translucent, add the pumpkin and salt. Stir a few times. Remove from heat.
- Add the coconut milk and vinegar to the pumpkin. Mix well and serve.

Pumpkin Flower Salad (Duddiya Kole Saasam)

Serves 4

INGREDIENTS

Pumpkin flowers, finely-chopped 36

Ridge gourd (torai), skinned and chopped 125 g

Sugar ½ tsp

MASALA

Half a coconut, roughly chopped

Tamarind 1-inch ball

Dry red chillies, roasted 1-5

Mustard seeds ¼ tsp

Asafoetida (hing) powder ¼ tsp

Water 4 tbsp

Salt to taste

METHOD

- Steam the pumpkin flowers till cooked.
- Steam the ridge gourd pieces separately till done. Mix with the pumpkin flowers.
- Grind the coconut, tamarind, red chillies, mustard and asafoetida together to a smooth paste with the water. Add salt to taste.
- Add the masala to the cooked pumpkin flower and ridge gourd and mix well. Serve hot or cold.

Tip: You can substitute the ridge gourd with 1 cup of cucumber pieces.

Maska Phulla Saasam is a variation of this dish, where pumpkin flowers are replaced with 1 lightly-packed cup of drumstick flowers boiled in 4 cups of water till soft, then drained.

Cucumber Salad (Keera Kosambari)

Serves 4

INGREDIENTS

4-inch cucumbers, grated 2

Coconut, grated 2 tbsp

Green chillies 1-2

Boiled water 1 tbsp

Yoghurt 2/3 cup

Salt to taste

SEASONING

Oil 1 tsp

Mustard seeds ¼ tsp

A pinch of asafoetida (hing) powder

METHOD

- Squeeze the water out of the grated cucumber and discard.
- Use a mortar and pestle to grind the green chillies with water. Strain to remove juice and set this aside.
- Add the grated coconut, chilli juice and salt to the grated cucumber.
- Heat the oil and fry the mustard seeds till they pop, adding the asafoetida (hing) for a few seconds at the end. When it releases its fragrance, pour this seasoning over the cucumber mix. Serve with vegetables and staples.

Tip: You can use onion, ridge gourd (torai), pumpkin or papaya instead of cucumber. Chop the vegetables into tiny pieces and steam till tender. Mix with the rest of the ingredients and season as above.

Kohl Rabi Salad (Knol Kohl Koshambari)

Serves 4

INGREDIENTS

Kohl Rabi (Navalkola), cut into small pieces
4 heaped tbsp

Salt 1 tsp

Coconut, grated 2 tbsp

SEASONING

Oil 2 tsp

Mustard seeds ¼ tsp

Cumin seeds ¼ tsp

Garlic cloves, crushed (optional) 8

Red chilli powder (optional) ½ tsp

Yoghurt 1 cup

Lime juice 1 tsp

Salt to taste

METHOD

- Crush the salt and kohl rabi pieces together. Squeeze, remove and discard water from the kohl rabi.
- Add the coconut to the kohlrabi.
- Heat the oil and fry the mustard, cumin, garlic and chilli powder. Add the kohl rabi coconut mixture, cover and cook over low heat till soft. Remove from heat and allow it to cool.
- Add yoghurt, lime juice and salt to taste. Mix well and serve.

Plantain Pith Salad (Gabbo Hasi)

INGREDIENTS

Plantain pith (4-inch long stem), minced 1

Salt to taste

Dosa chutney (Page 152)

METHOD

- Add a pinch of salt to the minced plantain pith (stem) and shake well. Let it stand for a few minutes and squeeze out and discard any water.
- Mix with all the dosa chutney and serve cold.

Tip: Substitute the plantain pith with 1 cup finely-chopped ridge gourd (torai).

Mango Salad

Serves 4-6

INGREDIENTS

Unripe mangoes (medium-sized), grated
2 pieces (roughly 200 g)

Thick coconut milk (Page 18) 4 tbsp

Yoghurt 2 tbsp

A big pinch of asafoetida (hing) powder

Green chillies, crushed with 1 tsp boiled
water 1-2

Sea salt ¼ tsp

Vegetable oil 1 tsp

METHOD

- Mix the grated mango, coconut milk, yoghurt and asafoetida together.
- Use a pestle and mortar to crush the green chillies and salt, then add water and crush some more. Strain the liquid and add to the mango mixture.
- Add the oil and mix well.

A tart, refreshing salad with a hint of chilli.

Carrot Salad (Kerete Koshambari)

Serves 4

INGREDIENTS

Carrots, peeled and finely-grated 6

Coconut, grated 6 level tbsp

Sugar ½ tsp

Salt to taste

SEASONING

Oil 3 tbsp

Mustard seeds ½ tsp

Yellow (husked) moong dal, soaked for 30 minutes and drained 3 level tbsp

Cumin seeds, powdered ½ tsp

Black peppercorns, powdered 30

Onions (large), minced 2

Juice of 1 lime

METHOD

- Mix the grated carrot, coconut, sugar and salt.
- Heat the oil and fry the mustard seeds, then add the moong dal and fry till golden brown.
- Add the onion and fry till light brown.
- Finally, add the cumin and pepper powder, stir once in the oil and immediately pour this seasoning over the carrot mixture. Stir well and add the lime juice. Mix again before serving.

Fragrant Sweet Potato Salad

Serves 4

Sweet potato, skinned and cubed 500 g or 1 large piece

Tomatoes (medium-size), chopped 200 g or 2 pieces

Green chillies, slit 2

SEASONING

Ghee 2 tsp

Mustard seeds ½ tsp

Cloves, ground 6

Cinnamon stick 2-inch piece

Coconut milk 1 cup (ready-made or made from half a coconut)

METHOD

- Steam the sweet potato cubes till done.
- Cook the tomato and green chillies till soft. Mix the potato cubes with the tomato mixture.
- Heat the ghee and pop the mustard seeds. Remove from fire and immediately add the cinnamon and powdered cloves. Stir and pour over the potato-tomato mixture.
- Add the cup of coconut milk, bring to a boil and turn off the heat. Serve warm or cold.

Chayote Salad (Merokai Saasam)

Serves 2

INGREDIENTS

1 chayote (chow chow), skinned and cut into ½-inch cubes

Red chilli powder (optional) ¼ -½ tsp

Jaggery ½-inch piece

Salt to taste

MASALA

Coconut, grated 4 tbsp

Red chillies, roasted 1-2

Tamarind 1-inch ball

Mustard seeds ¼ tsp

Water 2/3 cup

SEASONING

Oil 1 tbsp

Mustard seeds ¼ tsp

Curry leaves 2 sprigs

METHOD

- Boil 1 cup of water, add the chilli powder, jaggery and salt as well as the chopped chayote. Cook till soft but not mushy, till the water has dried up.

- Grind the masala ingredients together with ⅔ cup water. Add to the cooked chayote.

- Heat the oil and fry the mustard seeds and curry leaves. Pour over the chayote mixture, stir well and serve when cold.

Vegetables

Tender Cashewnut with Coconut Garnish (Bibbe Upkari)

Serves 4

INGREDIENTS

Tender cashewnuts 2 cups

Coconut, grated 4 tbsp

Salt to taste

SEASONING

Vegetable oil or ghee 4 tsp

Mustard seeds ½ tsp

Dry red chillies, broken into bits 3-6

Asafoetida (hing) powder ¼ tsp

METHOD

- Heat the oil and fry the mustard seeds, red chillies and asafoetida. Add the cashewnuts and cook over a low flame, tossing gently for 10 minutes.

- Add the grated coconut and salt and continue to cook for 3 minutes more. (You can also use the coconut as a garnish instead of roasting it.) Serve with chapatis or puris.

Tip: Tender cashews are generally available in the Konkan area in April and in August, when the cashew tree fruits. The thin, hard, pink-brown skin is peeled off after soaking, and then cooked in this delicious preparation.

If tender cashewnuts are not available, you can use the dried version. Soak in water for an hour or so before cooking.

To increase the quantity of this dish, you can add 12 cooked gherkins, sliced length-wise.

Malabar Cucumber (Magge Bendhi)

Serves 4

INGREDIENTS

Malabar cucumber, peeled and
chopped 4 cups

SEASONING

Coconut oil 2 tbsp

Mustard seed ½ tsp

Curry leaves 2 sprigs

MASALA

Coconut, grated 4 tbsp

Dry red chillies, roasted 1-2

1 lime-sized ball of tamarind

Water ¾ cup

Salt to taste

METHOD

- Steam or boil the cucumber pieces in very little water. Transfer the cooked pieces to a kadhai.

- In a small pan, heat oil and fry the mustard seeds and curry leaves. Pour this seasoning over the cucumber.

- Grind the coconut, red chillies and tamarind into a paste with a tablespoon or two of the water.

- Add the paste, salt and remaining water to the cucumber and bring it to a boil. Simmer for 5 minutes, and serve hot.

Tip: Magge has a firm texture compared to ordinary cucumber and holds its shape if cooked well. Since the water content is very high, it must be steamed for not more than 10 minutes. Do not pressure cook.

For seasoning, you can peel and crush 15 cloves of garlic and fry in vegetable oil instead of mustard seeds and curry leaves.

Coconut Okra (Bhend Sagle)

Serves 4

INGREDIENTS

Okra, topped and tailed 250 g

Water 2 tbsp

Salt to taste

SEASONING

Vegetable oil 1 tbsp

A pinch of mustard seeds

Curry leaves 1 sprig

MASALA

Vegetable oil ½ tsp

Coriander seeds 1 tsp

Fenugreek (methi) seeds ½ tsp

One-third of a small coconut

Red chillies, roasted 1-2

Tamarind ¾-inch ball

Water 1 cup

METHOD

- Heat the oil in a kadhai and fry the mustard seeds and curry leaves. Immediately add the okra. Cover and cook till tender, tossing occasionally. This takes about 10 minutes.

- In another pan, roast the red chillies till brown and set aside.

- Heat oil in the pan and fry the coriander and fenugreek seeds. Grind in a blender along with the coconut, chillies and tamarind to make a rough paste. Add the water and continue grinding till smooth.

- Stir the masala into the okra, bring to a boil and simmer for 5 minutes. Serve hot.

Tip: Sagle is the Konkani term for 'used whole'. Use aubergine, green peppers, gherkins or a mix of Malabar cucumbers and tender cashewnuts instead of okra.

Snake Gourd Curry (Poddaale Curry)

Serves 4-6

INGREDIENTS

Snake gourd (padwal), peel and chop into small ½-inch pieces 250 g or 3 cups

Ginger, grated 1½ tsp

Water 2¼ cups

Potato, peeled and cut into small cubes 200 g or 1½ cup

MASALA

Green chillies, chopped 1-3

Coconut, grated 1 tbsp

Turmeric ¾ tsp

SEASONING

Oil 3 tbsp

Mustard seeds 1½ tsp

Onion (small), finely-chopped 1

Salt 1 tsp

Red chilli powder (optional) ½ tsp

METHOD

- Bring the water to a boil and add the grated ginger and gourd. Boil till cooked but not mushy. Drain and reserve the water.
- Boil the potatoes till done. Drain.
- Grind the green chillies, coconut and turmeric into a coarse paste with a mortar and pestle or in a blender. Use 3 tablespoons of the reserved cooking water to remove all masala paste from the blender and keep aside.
- In a pan, heat the oil and fry the mustard seeds till they pop. Add the onions and fry till soft over a medium flame. Add the chilli powder and fry a little more.
- Add the green chilli, turmeric and coconut paste and fry together with the onion till brown, for about 10 minutes, over a low fire, stirring constantly.
- Now add the cooked gourd and potato pieces as well as the masala water and the salt. Cook for 10 minutes more, stirring gently as before. Serve hot with dosa, rice, idli or parathas.

Tip: You can use ash gourd (petha), ridge gourd (torai), gherkins (kundru) or plantain pith instead of the snake gourd.

Potato & Onions with Tamarind Masala (Batate Song)

Serves 4

INGREDIENTS

Potatoes (medium-sized) 6

Salt to taste

MASALA

Oil 2 tsp

Fenugreek seeds ½

Coriander seeds 2 heaped tsp

Coconut, grated 2 tbsp

Dry red chillies, roasted 2-4

Tamarind 1-inch ball

SEASONING

Oil 2 tbsp

Onions (medium-sized), finely chopped 2

METHOD

- Boil the potatoes, cool, peel and cut into cubes. Add the salt to the potato cubes and mix well.
- Heat oil in a pan and fry the fenugreek and coriander seeds till brown.
- Grind the seeds into a paste along with the coconut, red chillies and tamarind in a mixer.
- Heat oil in a kadhai and fry the onions till soft and golden brown.
- Combine the potato cubes and masala paste and add to the browned onions. Cook over a low flame for 10 minutes stirring from time to time. Serve with puris or chapatis.

Onion Curry (Piyavu Bhuthy)

Serves 4

INGREDIENTS

Onions (large), chopped into ½-inch bits
4 or 400 g

SEASONING

Vegetable oil 2 tsp

Mustard seeds ½ tsp

Onion (small), finely-chopped 1

MASALA

Oil ¼ tsp

Coriander seeds 1 tsp

Whole urad dal (husked black gram)
2 tsp

One-fourth coconut, roughly chopped
or grated

Dry red chillies, broken (optional) 3

Tamarind 1-inch ball or tamarind paste
1 tsp

Ginger 1-inch piece

Jaggery or sugar ½ tsp

Water 3 tbsp

Salt to taste

METHOD

- Steam or boil the 400 g chopped onions in just enough water to cook till translucent and tender.
- In a pan, heat the oil and pop the mustard seeds. Fry one finely chopped onion in the same oil and pour over the cooked onions.
- Roast the coriander seeds and dal in very little oil.
- Grind the coriander-dal mixture into a paste with coconut, chillies, tamarind and ginger in a mixer or with a mortar and pestle.
- Add the masala paste to the onions and mix well.
- Add the sugar, salt and water and stir a few times. Cook over a low fire for 10 minutes, then serve hot with chapatis or rice.

Tip: Replace the onions with 2 cups of drumstick flowers without stalks and 1 small brinjal cut into long pieces or tendli (kundru). If using tendli, cut it into rounds/circles.

Seasoned Gherkin Vegetable (Thendle Thalasani)

Serves 4

INGREDIENTS

Tender gherkins (kundru) 4 cups or
500 g

Salt to taste

A pinch of sugar or jaggery

SEASONING

Oil 1 tbsp

Dry red chillies, broken into bits 6

Garlic, skinned and crushed lightly 1
small pod

METHOD

- Top and tail the kundru. With a pestle or rolling pin crush each piece lightly to flatten, without breaking it into pieces. Add salt. Shake well for a while.
- Heat oil in a non-stick pan and add the crushed garlic. Stir till the garlic is lightly fried. Add the red chilli pieces and stir till fried.
- Add the kundru, salt and sugar. Cover and cook for 3 minutes till the vegetable is almost cooked. Stir constantly over a medium flame till the vegetables become a moderate brown. Serve hot.

Pigeon Peas & Mixed Vegetables (Kootu)

Serves 4 to 6

INGREDIENTS

Tur dal (pigeon pea lentils) 4 tbsp

Water 3 cups

Mixed vegetables 600 g or 4 cups (see tip below)

Water 4 cups

Curry leaves 30

Salt 1 tsp

MASALA

Half a fresh coconut

Dry red chillies 4

Cumin seeds 1 tsp

Water 2 cups

SEASONING

Vegetable oil 2 tsp

Mustard seeds ½ tsp

Whole urad dal (husked black gram) ½ tsp

Dry red chillies, broken into bits 2

METHOD

- Bring 3 cups water to a boil. Wash the dal, and pour it into the boiling water. Cook till soft but not mushy, about 15 minutes.

- Steam or boil the vegetables in 4 cups water with the salt and curry leaves till cooked. Drain.

- Grind the coconut, red chillies and cumin seeds till fine in a mixer. Add 2 cups water to make a paste.

- Add the masala and vegetables to the cooked dal. Bring to a boil and simmer for 3 to 5 minutes. Remove from heat.

- Heat the teaspoon of oil and pop the mustard seeds, urad dal and red chillies. Temper the vegetable and masala mixture and stir well. Serve with chapatis or rice.

Tip: Use yam, cauliflower, beans, ash gourd (petha), cucumber and green banana in equal quantities for the mixed vegetables. Roast 2 teaspoon of grated coconut till medium brown and add to the preparation before seasoning.

You can substitute tuvar dal with chilka moong (husked split lentils) or chana dal (Bengal gram), and use fresh green chillies instead of dried red ones.

Green Banana in a Coconut & Red Chilli Sauce (Plantain Koot)

Serves 4 to 6

INGREDIENTS

Green bananas, finely-chopped 500 g or 4 cups

Vegetable oil for deep frying 2 cups

MASALA

Fenugreek (methi) seeds ½ tsp

Mustard seeds ½ tsp

Asafoetida (hing) powder ¼ tsp

Turmeric powder ¼ tsp

Tamarind, without seeds 1-inch ball

Half a coconut, roughly-chopped

Red Byedgi chillies, roasted 4-8

Boiled water 1 cup

METHOD

- Make a slit along the length of the banana and remove the peel. Cut the banana in four pieces, length-wise, then chop into small bits about ½-inch in size. Wash the pieces well, sprinkle with salt and set aside for half an hour. Drain any water that collects in the pan.

- Heat the oil in a kadhai and fry the banana pieces in four batches till crisp and light brown in colour. Remove and drain on a kitchen towel.

- Drain the oil, reserving 2 teaspoons in the kadhai. Fry the fenugreek and mustard seeds till they pop.

- Remove the pan from the heat and add turmeric and asafoetida to the oil. Stir and pour into a mixer along with the coconut pieces, roasted chillies, tamarind and a quarter of the water. Blend, slowing adding the rest of the water till a smooth paste is made.

- Combine the fried banana pieces and the paste and serve hot.

Tip: Byedgi chillies are hotter than Kashmiri chillies and have a smokier flavour, so use per your heat preference.

Okra with Mustard Seeds (Bhend Upkari)

Serves 4 to 6

INGREDIENTS

Tender okra, cleaned and cut 500 g

Water 2 tbsp

Salt to taste

SEASONING

Vegetable oil 4 tsp

Mustard seed 1 tsp

Green chillies, deseeded and minced 3 to 6

Asafoetida (hing) powder ½ tsp

METHOD

- Wash and dry the okra thoroughly on kitchen towels. Top, tail and cut into 1-inch pieces.

- Take a kadhai and heat over medium flame. Add the okra, salt and water and toss them together in the pan.

- Heat the oil in a vagharia or small frying pan and pop the mustard seeds. Now fry the chillies and add the asafoetida powder to the same pan. When you can smell the scent of the asafoetida, the seasoning is ready.

- Pour the seasoning over the okra pieces. Cover tightly and cook the okra on a low heat till done – about 15 minutes. Stir from time to time during cooking before serving.

Spicy Corn (Jolu Upkari)

Serves 4

INGREDIENTS

Corn niblets 350 g

Green chillies, slit 2

A pinch of pepper powder

A pinch of asafoetida (hing) powder

A pinch of turmeric powder

A pinch of sugar

Coconut, grated 1 tbsp

Water 1 cup

SEASONING

Vegetable oil 1 tsp

Mustard seed ½ tsp

Juice of 1 lime

Salt to taste

METHOD

- Combine the corn, green chillies, spice powders, sugar and coconut together and boil in water till soft. This takes about 8 minutes.
- Heat oil in a small pan, and pop the mustard seeds. Pour the seasoning over the corn mixture. Stir and cook the corn for a further 5 minutes. Take off the heat and mix in lime juice and salt. Serve.

Tip: This works best as a snack or salad. To retain the freshness of the ingredients, add the grated coconut as garnish at the end instead of cooking it with the corn. Top with chopped coriander leaves.

Baby Potatoes in an Onion & Tomato Gravy

Serves 4

Baby potatoes, boiled, cooled and peeled 400 g

Red chilli powder (to taste)

Onions (large), chopped 2

Tomatoes, puréed 2

SEASONING

Oil 1 tbsp

A pinch of mustard seeds

A pinch of asafoetida (hing) powder

Salt to taste

METHOD

- Prick the boiled potatoes all over with a fork to make small holes. Sprinkle chilli powder over the potatoes.
- Heat oil in a kadhai and add the asafoetida and mustard seeds. When they pop, add the onions and fry till they are soft. Add the potatoes and fry for 10 minutes, stirring.
- Add the tomato juice and salt. Simmer for 15 minutes and serve hot.

Wild or Chinese Potatoes (Kook Upkari)

Serves 2 to 4

INGREDIENTS

Wild potatoes (kook) 24 (can be
substituted with 4 potatoes)

Salt to taste

SEASONING

Vegetable oil 2 tbsp

Cumin seeds ¼ tsp

Onions (large), chopped 2

Huli Powder (page 24) 2 tsp

METHOD

- Wash and scrub the wild potatoes till the water runs clear.

- Boil the will potatoes till they are cooked, but not mushy. Cool, peel and then cut them into four pieces each.

- Heat the oil. Fry the cumin seeds and onions till light brown. Add the Huli powder to the oil and stir while frying. Add the potatoes and cook over low heat for 10 minutes. Serve hot.

Tip: Chinese potato or kook as it's called in Konkani are root vegetables found in Mangalore and Bengaluru. The blackened skin of the kook can be cleaned first with a rough cloth, then by soaking, washing and scrubbing them very well.

To skin kook, use a peeler or pressure cook them for a minute at high pressure. Peel immediately on removing from heat.

Wash them thoroughly in water and slice them length-wise. Soak the pieces in water to prevent them from discolouring and turning brown.

Pumpkin & Green Gram Curry (Alchakari)

Serves 4

INGREDIENTS

Whole moong (whole green gram), soaked overnight ½ cup

Pumpkin, diced 250 g

Bilimbis (also known as bimbla fruit, a sour seasonal fruit from Goa), slit 2 (optional)

Coconut, grated 1

Dry red chillies, roasted 4-6

Turmeric ½ tsp

Water 2 cups

Salt to taste

SEASONING

Vegetable oil 1 tbsp

Mustard seeds ½ tsp

Cumin seeds ½ tsp

Curry leaves 2 sprigs

METHOD

- Cook the green gram in water till soft.
- Roast 4 tablespoons of coconut over low heat till light brown.
- In a mixer, grind the rest of the coconut with the red chillies, turmeric and just enough water to make a smooth paste.
- In a pan, mix the paste with the green gram, diced pumpkin, bilimbi, salt and roasted coconut.
- Heat the oil in a separate pan and fry the mustard seeds till they pop. Add the cumin and curry leaves. Stir till fried.
- Heat the green gram and pumpkin mixture and pour the seasoning over it. Stir well, bring the vegetable to a boil and cook for 10 minutes till the pumpkin is tender.

Note: This dish is often served during religious ceremonies. You can substitute tuvar (pigeon pea) dal for the green gram and yam (suran) for the pumpkin.

Aubergine Curry (Gulla Bajji)

Serves 4 to 6

INGREDIENTS

Small aubergines, cut into 1-inch long pieces 500 g

SEASONING

Vegetable oil 1½ tbsp

Mustard seeds ½ tsp

Cumin seeds ½ tsp

Fenugreek seeds ¼ tsp

Coriander seeds 1 tsp

Garam masala powder (page 23) ½ tsp

Turmeric powder ½ tsp

Coconut, grated 2 tbsp

Water 2 tbsp

Tomatoes, chopped 2

Onions, chopped 2

METHOD

- Put the aubergines in a kadhai.
- Heat the oil in a small pan and fry the mustard seeds, cumin, fenugreek and coriander seeds. Add the garam masala and turmeric powder last, give it a stir and pour over the aubergines.
- Cover and cook over a low flame till the aubergines are almost tender.
- Add the coconut and water and continue to cook for another 5 minutes.
- Add the tomatoes, onions and salt. Cover and cook till onions are soft. Mix well and serve.

Tip: This dish is traditionally prepared with Gool or Gulla, a round, green variety of aubergines which grow in the Udupi region during January and February.

Chow Chow with Onions (Merokai Upkari)

Serves 4

INGREDIENTS

Chow chow (chayotes) 4

Salt ½ tsp

SEASONING

Vegetable oil 2 tbsp

Mustard seeds 1 tsp

Onions (medium), chopped 4

Red chilli powder 1 tsp

Coconut, grated 4 tbsp

METHOD

- Wash and coarsely grate the chow chow.
- Heat the oil and fry the mustard seeds and onions. When the onions soften, add the chilli powder and stir.
- Add the chow chow. Cover and cook over low heat without adding any water. Stir frequently, and remove from heat when soft. Garnish with coconut and serve.

Tip: Chow chow is a pear-shaped gourd commonly used in Konkani cooking. In this recipe, it can be substituted with one medium-sized papaya.

Sprouted Green Gram (Gram Sukke)

Serves 4-6

INGREDIENTS

Whole moong (whole green gram), sprouted 125 g (page 18)

Potatoes 200 g

Water 1 ltr

Salt to taste

SEASONING

Vegetable oil 2 tsp

Mustard seeds ½ tsp

Curry leaves 2 sprigs

MASALA

Oil 1 tsp

Urad dal (husked black gram) 1 tsp

Coriander seeds 1 tsp

One-fourth of a coconut

Dry red chillies, roasted 2

Tamarind ½-inch ball

METHOD

- Boil 1 litre of water and add washed, sprouted gram. Boil till soft.
- Boil the potatoes till done. Peel and cut into 1-inch cube.
- Heat 1 tsp of oil and pop the mustard seeds. Add the curry leaves, fry, then add the sprouts and potatoes. Stir for a minute, then add salt to taste.
- Heat oil in another pan and fry the urad dal. Remove from oil, then use the same oil to fry the coriander seeds till golden brown.
- Grind the fried coriander and urad dal in a mixer with the coconut, roasted red chillies and tamarind. Slowly, add 1 cup of water to the mixer and grind to a fine thin paste.
- Pour the paste over the seasoned gram and potatoes. Mix well, bring to a boil and cook for 5 minutes till very little liquid remains. Serve hot with rice or parathas.

Tip: You can substitute the sprouted moong and potato with jackfruit, green bananas, cluster beans and tender bamboo shoots.

Green Beans with Onion

Serves 4 to 6

INGREDIENTS

Green beans 500 g

Coconut, grated 2 tbsp

Green chillies, finely chopped 2-4
(optional)

Salt to taste

SEASONING

Ghee or vegetable oil 4 tsp

Mustard seeds ¼ tsp

Cumin seed ¼ tsp

Onion (large), finely chopped 1

Besan (gram flour) 2 tsp

Turmeric ¼ tsp

Red chilli powder (optional) ¼ tsp

METHOD

- Chop the beans into ½-inch pieces. Steam with the chillies till almost cooked.
- Transfer the beans and chillies to a kadhai. Add the coconut and salt. Mix well.
- Heat the ghee in a small pan and pop the mustard and cumin seeds.
- Add the onions and fry till soft, then add the besan and fry till brown.
- Add the turmeric and chilli powder and stir for a few seconds. Pour over the beans and cook, stirring frequently, over medium heat for 10 minutes. Serve hot with chapatis or parathas.

Banana Flower Curry (Bondi Curry)

Serves 4 to 6

INGREDIENTS

Plantain flower 1 (or 400 g)

SEASONING

Ghee or vegetable oil 1 tbsp

Mustard seeds ½ tsp

Green chillies, finely-chopped 2

Asafoetida (hing) powder ¼ tsp

Red chilli powder ½ tsp

MASALA

One-fourth of a coconut

Tamarind ½-inch ball

Coriander seeds 1 heaped tsp

Water 4 tbsp

Jaggery or sugar 1 tsp

Salt to taste

METHOD

- With oiled hands (see tip below), remove the purplish-maroon outer leaves of the banana flower. The flowers with stamens are on the inside of the leaves. Remove the flower and set aside. Discard any which are black or badly discoloured. Keep removing the leaves and picking the flowers. When you get to the inner core, which is light green to white in colour, keep the leaves and chop along with the flowers. This should make about 4 to 5 cups or 400 g of flowers and leaves. **Note:** The stamens of the flowers must be removed before chopping the flowers or the dish will taste bitter.

- Sprinkle salt on the flowers, set aside for 15 minutes and then wash well. Keep the chopped flowers immersed in salt water to prevent them from turning brown or black.

- Steam the chopped flowers and leaves. When soft, remove from the heat and put into a kadhai.

- Heat the ghee in a frying pan and pop the mustard seeds. Add the green chillies and take off heat. Add the red chilli powder and asafoetida and stir. Pour this seasoning over the banana flowers.

- Grind the coconut, coriander seeds and tamarind in the water till a smooth paste is formed.

- Mix the masala paste with the banana flowers. Add the jaggery and salt, and cook over a low flame for 15 minutes, stirring often. Serve hot with chapatis or rice.

Tip: Banana blossoms are difficult to clean due to the black sap. Rubbing oil all over your hands before handling the blossom will prevent stains.

Breadfruit Curry (Jeev Kadgi Song)

Serves 4

INGREDIENTS

Breadfruit (jeev kadgi or fanas) 1 medium-sized or 250 g cubes

Asafoetida (hing) powder ¼ tsp

Besan (gram flour) 4 tbsp

Water ¼ cup

Vegetable oil 1 cup (for deep-frying)

Tomatoes (medium-sized), finely-chopped 3

Red chilli powder 1 tsp (optional)

Salt to taste

SEASONING

Oil 2 tbsp

Mustard seeds 1 tsp

Onions, finely-chopped 3

Green chillies, slit 2

Turmeric ½ tsp

Coconut milk 1 ½ cups (extracted from 1 coconut, page 18)

Red chilli powder ½ tsp (optional)

METHOD

- Quarter the breadfruit and remove the inner hard, white pith and skin. Cut into cubes. Keep the chopped fruit in a pan of water while cutting to prevent discolouration.

- Mix the chilli powder, asafoetida, besan and salt. Now, add the water to make a paste and marinate the breadfruit cubes into the paste.

- Heat the oil and fry breadfruit in 4-5 batches till brown and crisp.

- Heat 2 tbsp of oil and fry the mustard seeds, green chillies, onions, chilli powder and turmeric. When the onions are soft, add the tomatoes. Cover and cook till tender and mushy.

- Add the breadfruit pieces and coconut milk to the tomato spice mixture and stir well. Bring to a boil and simmer for 5 minutes. Serve hot.

Tip: When buying breadfruit, look for fruit which is dull green and not too soft. When making this dish, I like to add the fried breadfruit just before serving to retain the crunch. You can also add cooked peas to it.

For variation, substitute potato, cauliflower, kundru (gherkins) or snake gourd (padwal) for the breadfruit.

Potato Curry

Serves 4

INGREDIENTS

Potatoes (medium-sized) boiled, peeled and cut into cubes 6

A pinch of turmeric

Salt to taste

MASALA

Ginger, grated ¼ tsp

Garlic cloves, chopped 4

Green chillies, roughly-chopped 1-2

SEASONING

Vegetable oil 1 tbsp

Mustard seeds ¼ tsp

Onion (medium-sized), finely-chopped 1

Fresh coriander, finely-chopped 3 tbsp

Tomato, finely-chopped 1

MASALA 2

Oil 1 tbsp

Coconut, grated 2 tbsp

Cumin seeds ¼ tsp

Coriander seeds ½ tsp

Cloves 2

Cinnamon ¼-inch piece

Black peppercorns 6

Dry red chillies 1-3

Water 1 ½ cups

METHOD

- Make a paste of the ginger, green chillies and garlic with a mortar and pestle. Transfer to a kadhai.

- In another pan, heat the oil and fry the mustard seeds, onion and coriander. Pour over the ginger paste and cook for 3 minutes.

- Add the chopped tomato, cover and cook for 5 minutes till soft. Add the potato and cook for another 5 minutes, stirring constantly.

- To make Masala 2, fry the cumin, coriander, pepper, cloves, cinnamon, red chilli and grated coconut in oil and grind to a fine paste in a mixer.

- Add the masala to the potatoes along with 1½ cups of water. Cook for 10 minutes till the gravy thickens, then serve with chapatis or puris.

Tip: To reduce the pungency of this dish, adjust the quantity of green chillies, red chillies and pepper to your taste.

Garden Greens (Thotakoora Curry)

Serves 2 to 4

INGREDIENTS

Tender amaranth (chawli) stems, cut into 1-inch pieces 1 cup

Aubergine (medium-sized), cut into 2½-inch long pieces 1

Sugar ½ tsp

Salt to taste

MASALA

Vegetable oil 1 tsp

Green chillies 1-3

Mustard seeds 1 tsp

One-eighth of a fresh coconut, broken into bits

Tamarind 1-inch ball

Water 2/3 cup

A pinch of asafoetida (hing) powder

SEASONING

Vegetable oil 2 tsp

Mustard seeds ¼ tsp

Curry leaves 1 sprig

METHOD

- Boil the stems of the greens in 2 cups of water till soft. Drain.
- Boil the aubergine pieces in 3 cups of water for 8 minutes. Drain.
- Add the cooked stems, sugar and salt to the aubergine. Cook over a low flame till the aubergine is cooked.
- In another pan, fry the mustard seed, green chillies and asafoetida in oil.
- Grind the spices along with the coconut, tamarind and water in a mixer till smooth. Pour the ground ingredients on to the aubergine and stems curry. Turn heat down low. Do not allow to boil.
- To season, heat the oil and fry the mustard seeds and curry leaves. Pour the seasoning over the curry. Simmer for 5 minutes and serve hot.

Tip: Double the quantity if you are cooking only one vegetable for the meal.

Green Tomato Curry

Serves 2 to 4

INGREDIENTS

Green tomatoes, chopped 400 g

Jaggery or sugar ½ tsp

Salt ½ tsp

SEASONING

Oil ½ tbsp

Mustard seeds ¼ tsp

MASALA

Vegetable oil ½ tsp

Black peppercorns 12

Fenugreek (methi) seeds ¼ tsp

Urad dal (husked black gram) 2 heaped tsp

Dry red chillies, broken into bits 1-5 (optional)

A pinch of asafoetida (hing) powder

A pinch of turmeric powder

METHOD

- Heat ½ tbsp oil in a pan. Add mustard seeds. When they pop, pour over the chopped tomatoes. Add sugar and salt. Cover and cook, simmering without adding water.
- Meanwhile, heat oil in a pan for seasoning. Fry the peppercorns, fenugreek, lentils and red chillies separately in the oil. Remove from heat and add the turmeric and asafoetida.
- Make a powder of the fried spices in a coffee grinder.
- When the tomatoes are cooked and fairly dry, add the powdered masala and mix well. Cook for a few more minutes over low heat. Serve hot with rice or chapatis.

Tip: You can substitute the green tomatoes with green peppers (Shimla mirch). If you're using green peppers, add a little tamarind when grinding the spices to add tartness to the dish.

Apple Curry

Serves 4

INGREDIENTS

Sour green apples, cored, peeled and chopped 250 g

Jaggery or sugar 1 tsp

Water 3 tbsp

Salt ½ tsp

SEASONING

Ghee 1 tbsp

Mustard seeds ½ tsp

Cumin seeds ½ tsp

A pinch of fenugreek (methi) seeds

Pepper powder ¼ tsp

A big pinch of asafoetida (hing) powder

Turmeric powder ¼ tsp

MASALA

Coconut, grated 4 tbsp

Green chillies 2

Poppy seeds (khus khus) 2 tsp

Tamarind ½-inch ball or ½ tsp paste

METHOD

- Place the apple cubes in a pan along with the sugar, water and salt.
- In another pan, heat the ghee and fry the mustard, cumin and fenugreek. Take off the heat and add the asafoetida, pepper and cumin to the oil. Let it sizzle and then pour over the apples. Cook the mixture over a low flame till tender, for about 10 minutes, stirring occasionally. When the apple mixture is cooked, take the pan off the heat and let it cool a little
- Meanwhile dry roast the masala ingredients one by one over a low fire. Toast the grated coconut till light brown. Stir continuously to prevent burning and sticking. Remove from pan. Toast the poppy seeds till light brown as well. Remove from pan. Roast the green chillies last, till the green colour changes to brown spots.
- Grind the toasted masala with the tamarind in a mixer to make a fine paste. Add ¼ cup of boiled water and grind again to make a smooth paste.
- Combine the ground masala and apples, mix well and serve hot.

Tip: You can toast grated coconut in larger quantities and freeze to reduce the preparation time.

Mixed Vegetables with Green Chillies (Yogyarathna)

Serves 4

INGREDIENTS

Mixed vegetables, cut into pieces 3 cups

Green chillies, slit 6

Water 3 cups

SEASONING

Oil 1 tbsp

A pinch of mustard seeds

A pinch of cumin seeds

Curry leaves 1 sprig

A big pinch of asafoetida (hing) powder

Three-fourth of a coconut

Salt to taste

METHOD

- Boil the vegetables with the chillies in the water till tender. Drain.
- Heat the oil and fry the mustard and cumin seeds, the curry leaves and asafoetida. Pour over the cooked vegetables.
- Make coconut milk by grinding the coconut in a mixer with only ½ cup of water and strain. Alternatively, you can use 120 ml coconut milk.
- Add the coconut milk to the seasoned vegetables and simmer for 10 minutes. Add salt to taste.

Tip: You can use potatoes, peas, green beans, ash gourd (petha), lentils, ridge gourd (torai) and tender cashewnuts in equal quantities to make this vegetable dish.

Bitter Gourd (Karate)

Serves 4-6

INGREDIENTS

Bitter gourds (karela), seeded and cut into long 2-inch long pieces 2

Salt 1 tsp

Water 2 cups

Potatoes (medium-sized) 2

Colocasia (arvi) tubers 8

Bilimbis, split 2

Tamarind 1 lime-sized piece soaked in 2/3 cup water

Dry red chillies 1-6

Salt to taste

SEASONING

Oil 1 tbsp

Mustard seeds ½ tsp

Curry leaves 2 sprigs

METHOD

- Boil the bitter gourd pieces in 2 cups of salted water. Drain.
- Boil, cool, peel and cut the potatoes and tubers into ¾-inch cubes and mix with the gourd pieces.
- Strain the soaked tamarind to make tamarind juice and add to the vegetables along with the salt. Mix well.
- Make a paste of the red chillies with a mortar and pestle and add to the vegetables.
- Heat the oil and fry the mustard seeds and curry leaves. Pour over the vegetables, bring to a boil and simmer for 10 minutes. Serve hot.

Tangy Capsicum (Donne Mirsang)

Serves 2 to 4

INGREDIENTS

Capsicum (Shimla mirch), cut into 1-inch pieces 250 g

A pinch of sugar or jaggery

Salt to taste

SEASONING

Oil 2 tbsp

A pinch of mustard seeds

A pinch of fenugreek (methi) seeds

Red chilli powder ½ tsp (optional)

A pinch of asafoetida powder

A pinch of turmeric powder

Juice of 1 lime

METHOD

- Heat the oil in a pan. Add the mustard seeds and cook till they pop. Add the fenugreek seeds. Take the pan off the heat and stir in the chilli, asafoetida and turmeric.
- Add the capsicum, salt and sugar. Cover and cook over low heat till tender, about 8 minutes.
- Add the lime juice and stir well. Serve hot.

Tip: I make this without removing all the seeds from the green peppers and then cut out the red chilli powder. Add the lime juice at the end just before serving. This way the nutrients remain and the taste of lime is sharper.

You can substitute snake gourd (padwal) for capsicum, and use 1 tbsp of grated raw green mango instead of lime juice. Add the mango at the beginning with the sugar and salt.

Spinach Cake (Palak or Thotakoora Cake)

Serves 4

INGREDIENTS

Spinach leaves, washed, stemmed and chopped 1 bunch (4 cups of chopped spinach)

MASALA

Yellow moong dal (husked green gram), washed and soaked for an hour 1 heaped tbsp

Half a fresh coconut, roughly chopped

Byedgi chillies, roasted 2-6

Tamarind paste ½ tsp

A big pinch of asafoetida (hing) powder

SEASONING

Vegetable oil 2 tsp

Mustard seeds ¼ tsp

Salt to taste

METHOD

- Grind the soaked dal, coconut, red chillies, tamarind and asafoetida to make a batter. Do not add water.
- Heat the oil, sauté the mustard seeds and temper the batter with this seasoning.
- Add the chopped spinach leaves and salt to the batter and mix well.
- Pour the mixture into a 5-inch greased baking dish or pan and press down firmly to flatten. Steam in a double boiler till cooked for about 30-35 minutes. Cool, cut into slices or cubes and serve.

Tips: Use 4 cups of finely chopped amaranthus (chawli) leaves or 4 cups of drumstick flowers (boiled in 4 cups of water for 5 minutes) instead of the spinach. Steam for 40-45 minutes.

A savoury dish that can be served for breakfast, lunch or dinner

Cauliflower Curry

Serves 4

INGREDIENTS

Cauliflower florets and stems 400 g

Water 2 cups

Tomatoes, chopped 2

MASALA

Coriander seeds 4 tsp

Cumin seeds ½ tsp

Turmeric powder ¼ tsp

Fresh ginger ½-inch piece

Coconut, grated 2 tbsp

Black peppercorns 12

Garlic cloves 10

Dry red chilli 1

SEASONING

Vegetable oil 2 tbsp

Cinnamon 1-inch piece

Cloves 6

Onions, chopped fine 2

Water ½ cup

Salt to taste

METHOD

- Cut the cauliflower into medium-sized florets and remove the outer stringy part of the stems. Chop the stem into 1-inch pieces. Steam or boil the stems and florets in 2 cups of water till half cooked. Drain.

- Make a masala in the mixer with the coriander, cumin, turmeric, ginger, coconut, pepper, garlic and red chilli. Pour the masala into a pan.

- In another pan, heat the oil and fry the cinnamon, cloves and onions. Pour the seasoning over the masala paste.

- Over a low flame, cook the masala and seasoning till light brown. When it emits an aroma, add the chopped tomato, cover and cook for 5 to 7 minutes till the tomato is tender.

- Add the cauliflower and water, and cook for 10 minutes till the cauliflower is tender. Add salt to taste and serve with rice or chapatis.

Hot Potato Curry

Serves 4

INGREDIENTS

Potatoes (large), peeled and cut into cubes 3

Water 3 cups

Salt to taste

MASALA

Mustard seeds ¼ tsp

Coriander seeds 2 tbsp

Black peppercorns 12

Turmeric powder ¼ tsp

Asafoetida (hing) powder ¼ tsp

Half a coconut, roughly chopped

Dry red chillies 2 (optional)

Tamarind 1 lime-sized ball

Water 2 cups

SEASONING

Oil 2 tbsp

Mustard seeds 1 tsp

Curry leaves 3 sprigs

METHOD

- Cook the potato cubes with salt in the water till almost done. Drain.
- Grind the mustard seeds, coriander and peppercorns into a powder. Add these spices and the asafoetida and turmeric to the coconut, chillies and tamarind. Grind in a mixer adding just enough water to make a smooth paste.
- Add the masala paste to the cooked potatoes with 2 cups water.
- Heat the oil in another pan and fry the mustard seeds and curry leaves. Pour this seasoning over the potato and masala. Mix well and bring to a boil and simmer over low heat for 10 minutes. Serve hot with chapatis, parathas, dosas or rice.

Tip: You can substitute tamarind with 2 tbsp grated unripe mango, and use cabbage, cauliflower, snake gourd, cucumber or gherkins instead of potatoes.

Mixed Vegetable Curry (Gajbaj Upkari)

Serves 4

INGREDIENTS

Mixed vegetables 400 g

Green chillies, slit 2

Boiling water 3 cups

Tomato (medium-sized), finely-chopped 1

A pinch of turmeric powder

SEASONING

Oil 1 tbsp

Curry leaves 1 sprig

A pinch of mustard seeds

A pinch of asafoetida (hing) powder

MASALA

Half a coconut, roughly chopped

Dry red chillies, roasted 3

Water 2 tbsp

Salt to taste

METHOD

- Boil water, add the mixed vegetables and cook till soft. (They can also be steamed.) Reserve the water.

- Place the chopped tomatoes in a kadhai.

- Heat the oil and fry the mustard seeds, curry leaves and asafoetida. As soon as the asafoetida gives its distinctive smell, pour the seasoning over the chopped tomato. Cover and cook over low heat till the tomato gets soft.

- Meanwhile grind the coconut, roasted red chillies and water into a paste in a mixer.

- Add the cooked vegetables to the tomato mixture and then mix in the masala paste and salt.

- Add the 2 cups of water in which the vegetables were cooked and bring to a boil. Simmer for 10 minutes till the curry is thick and soupy but not dry. Serve hot with rice or chapatis.

Ash Gourd & Colocasia Curry (Koot Curry)

Serves 2-4

INGREDIENTS

Ash gourd (petha), diced 2 cups

Green chillies, slit length-wise and deseeded 2

Colocasia (arvi) tubers 3

Coconut milk 200 ml

Salt ½ tsp

Coconut oil 3 tsp

A big pinch of asafoetida powder

METHOD

- Steam or boil the petha and green chillies together till tender.
- Boil the tubers till done. Cool, peel and slice into ⅛-inch thick rounds.
- Add the sliced tubers, coconut milk and salt to the cooked petha. Bring to a boil and remove from heat.
- Stir in the coconut oil and asafoetida powder and serve.

Tip: Use a mix of potatoes, peas, beans, cucumber, kundru (gherkins) or pumpkin in place of the petha and colocasia tubers.

Lentils/Dal

Dalithoi

Serves 6

INGREDIENTS

Tuvar dal (pigeon pea lentils) 1⅓ cup

Water 5 cups

Large green chillies, slit and deseed 1-3 (to taste)

Fresh coriander leaves, finely chopped 1/3 cup

Ginger, lightly crushed ½-inch piece

Salt 1½ tsp

SEASONING

Vegetable oil 3 tsp

Mustard seeds 1 level tsp

Red chillies, roughly torn 1-2 (optional)

Curry leaves 2 sprigs

Asafoetida (hing) ¼ tsp

METHOD

- Wash the lentils till the water runs clear and set aside.
- In a saucepan, bring water to a boil. Add the washed dal and bring it to a boil again. Reduce heat to medium and cook, half covered, for 10 minutes.
- Add the chillies and ginger to the dal and cook, almost completely covered, for another 10 minutes. Turn heat to low. Stir in the salt and chopped coriander leaves.
- Heat the oil in a small non-stick pan. Add the mustard seeds and as they pop, add the red chillies and curry leaves. Pour over dal and remove the pan from heat.

Tip: When yellow moong dal (husked moong) or lal masoor dal (split red lentils) are substituted for tuvar, use only 125 g. You can also finely chop 4 tomatoes and add along with the green chillies to make an interesting and tasty variation.

Comfort food from the Konkan region, this dal is served most frequently in Saraswat homes with spicy vegetables like Batate Song for a balanced combination of flavours.

Masoor with Chow Chow & Fenugreek (Belehuli)

Serves 4

INGREDIENTS

Masoor dal (red lentils) ⅓ cup

Green chillies 6

SEASONING

Ghee 1 tbsp

Fenugreek seeds 1 tsp

Chow chow (chayote), peeled, chopped and boiled ½ piece

Red chilli powder ¼ tsp

Jaggery (gur) 1 tsp

Pulp of ½-inch tamarind

Curry leaves 1 sprig

A handful coriander leaves, chop

A pinch asafoetida (hing) powder

Salt to taste

METHOD

- Wash the dal. Bring 3 cups of water to boil and add the dal and the whole green chillies. Boil till soft.
- Heat the ghee and fry the fenugreek seeds. Pour this seasoning over the cooked dal.
- Add the steamed chow chow to the dal along with the chilli powder, jaggery, tamarind pulp, curry leaves, coriander leaves, asafoetida and salt.
- Bring this mixture to a boil and reduce heat to simmer for about 8 minutes. Serve with rice or parathas.

Cumin & Black Pepper Dal (Jeera Dal)

Serves 2

INGREDIENTS

Tuvar dal (pigeon pea lentils) 65 g

Water ½ litre

Green beans, sliced length-wise 75 g

Long green chillies, slit length wise 1-2 (optional)

Vegetable oil 2 tsp

Black peppercorns 10

Cumin ½ tsp

Salt to taste

SEASONING

Vegetable oil 1 tsp

Mustard seeds 1 tsp

Curry leaves 1 sprig

Juice from half a lime

METHOD

- Wash the dal and set aside. In a pan, bring water to a boil and add the washed dal. Cook till half done for about 20 minutes.

- Add the green beans and chillies to the dal and cook till both the dal and beans are done – about 15 minutes more.

- Heat 1 tsp of oil and fry the peppercorns on low heat. Remove the pepper from the oil and fry the cumin seeds till they pop. Grind pepper and cumin seeds together till fine. Add the spice mix to the dal along with salt and cook for an additional 5-8 minutes. Remove from heat.

- Heat the second tsp of oil, pop the mustard seeds and fry the curry leaves. Pour this seasoning over the dal. Add the juice of half a lime and serve hot.

Tip: Use an equal quantity of small aubergines or gherkins instead of the green beans.

A slightly sour dal to balance the pungency of the pepper.

Mango Dal

Serves 4

INGREDIENTS

Tuvar dal (pigeon pea lentils) 75 g

Water 3 cups

Unripe green mango (kairee), minced 1 tbsp

Green chillies, slit and deseed 1-3 (optional)

Salt to taste

MASALA

Ghee 1 tsp

Garlic cloves, crushed 6

Coconut, grated 1 tbsp

Coriander leaves, roughly chopped 1 cup

Water ½ cup

SEASONING

Vegetable oil 2 tsp

Mustard seeds 1 tsp

Cumin seeds ¼ tsp

Curry leaves 1 sprig

A pinch of asafoetida (hing) powder

METHOD

- Wash the dal. In a pan, bring the water to a boil and add the washed dal. Cook for 30 minutes or till it is three-quarters cooked and almost translucent.
- Add the minced mango, green chillies and salt. Boil for an additional 5 minutes till the mango becomes soft.
- Heat the oil and fry the garlic, then let it cool.
- Make a paste of the garlic, coconut and coriander leaves in a mixer with the water.
- Add the masala paste and 500 ml water to the cooked dal and bring the quantity up to 4 cups or 1 litre. Bring to a boil and cook for 5 minutes.
- Fry the seasoning in a small pan or vagharia and pour over the cooked dal. Mix well and serve hot with steamed rice.

Red Lentil & Garlic Dal (Masoor Saar)

Serves 4 to 6

INGREDIENTS

Masoor dal (whole red lentils) ½ cup

Boiling water 6 cups

Two handfuls of green coriander leaves, finely-chopped

Tamarind 1 marble-sized piece

Sugar ¼ tsp

Salt ½ tsp

SEASONING

Vegetable oil 2 tsp

Mustard seeds ½ tsp

Garlic, skinned and crushed 1 pod or 20 cloves

Dried red chillies, broken into bits 3-5

A big pinch of asafoetida (hing) powder

METHOD

- Wash the dal and cook in water for an hour, until it softens and the skins split. Strain through a fine wire strainer and discard the skins.

- Soak the tamarind in 2 tbsp of hot water. Strain the pulp and mix into the dal. Simmer on low heat.

- Add the coriander, sugar and salt. Mix well and keep cooking the dal. Add sufficient water so it measures 4 cups of dal.

- Heat the oil in a pan and add the seasoning ingredients in the order listed: mustard seeds, garlic cloves, red chillies and asafoetida. As the spices crackle and pop, pour the seasoning over the cooked dal. Serve hot with rice or chapatis. (This dal keeps well for several days.)

Moong Dal (Varan)

Serves 4

INGREDIENTS

Moong dal (husked green gram)125 g

Water ½ litre

Mild green chillies, slit 6

MASALA

Half a coconut, grated

Cumin seeds ½ tsp

Turmeric powder ¼ tsp

Salt to taste

SEASONING

Vegetable oil or ghee 1-2 tbsp

Mustard seeds 1 tsp

Curry leaves 2 sprigs

Juice of half a lime

METHOD

- Wash the dal. In a saucepan, bring water to a boil and add the dal and chillies. Cook for about 20 minutes till the dal softens.
- Grind the coconut, cumin seeds and turmeric to a smooth paste. Add 1 cup of water and salt, and pour the mixture into the cooked dal. Bring the dal back to a boil and cook on low heat for 5 minutes.
- Heat the oil in a small pan, fry the mustard seeds till they pop. Add and fry curry leaves and pour over the dal.
- Stir in the lime juice and serve hot.

Mangalorean Sambar
(Spicy Lentils with Mixed Vegetables)

Serves 8

INGREDIENTS

Tuvar dal (pigeon pea lentils) 200 g

Water 1½ litres

Mixed vegetables, cut into large cubes
2-3 cups

Mangalore sambar powder 1½ tsp
(page 25)

Tamarind pulp ¾ tsp

Salt 1 tsp

Jaggery 1 tsp (optional)

SEASONING

Oil 1 tbsp

Mustard seeds 1 tsp

Curry leaves 2 sprigs

Coriander leaves, finely-chopped
1-2 tbsp

METHOD

- Wash the dal. In a saucepan, bring water to a boil and add the dal. Cook for 20 minutes till half done.

- Add the cleaned and cut vegetables to the dal and continue to cook till soft, for about 20 minutes.

- Add the sambar powder, tamarind paste, jaggery and salt and continue to cook for 10 more minutes.

- Heat the oil in a small pan and fry the mustard seeds till they pop. Add the curry leaves and fry for another few seconds. Pour over the dal and vegetable mixture. Garnish with coriander leaves and serve hot with rice.

Tip: You can use shallots, aubergine, potato, ash gourd, tomato, beans, drumsticks and turnips for this dish.

Morkolambu

Serves 2

INGREDIENTS

Ash gourd (petha) pieces, 300 g

Green chillies, slit and deseed 2-3

Turmeric ¼ tsp

Water ¼ cup

Half a fresh coconut, scraped or cut into pieces

Water ½ cup

Salt to taste

SEASONING

Vegetable oil 1 tbsp

Mustard seeds 1 tsp

Cumin ½ tsp

Black peppercorns, crushed 8

Curry leaves 2 sprigs

Buttermilk 2 cups

METHOD

- Cook the petha with the green chillies and turmeric in just enough water till soft.
- Grind the coconut in a blender with the salt and half a cup water to form a smooth paste.
- Add the paste to the cooked petha. Bring to a boil and simmer on low heat for 5 minutes.
- Heat oil in a small pan and pop the mustard seeds, cumin and crushed peppercorns. Add the curry leaves and fry for a few seconds. Pour over the cooked gourd and mix gently.
- Remove from heat and allow the preparation to cool. Stir in the buttermilk, stir well and serve.

Tip: The buttermilk can sour after a couple of hours. If there is a gap between preparation and serving, bring the curry to a boil after adding the buttermilk to the petha. The buttermilk may split but the taste will remain unchanged.

You can substitute the petha with lauki (bottle gourd), cucumber or kundru (gherkins).

A tangy soup-like curry.

Lentil Dumpling Dal (Parpurande Kolambu)

Serves 8

INGREDIENTS

DUMPLINGS

Tuvar dal (pigeon pea lentils) 150 g

Red chilli powder 1 tsp

Salt 1 tsp

A big pinch of asafoetida (hing) powder

Water 3 tbsp

Grated coconut 2 heaped tbsp

Onion, minced 2 heaped tsp

Coconut oil 2 tsp

Coriander leaves, chopped
2 heaped tsp

Rice flour, 1 heaped tsp

GRAVY

1½-inch diameter tamarind ball or
tamarind pulp 1 tsp

Water 1½ cups

Sambar powder (page 25) or Huli
powder (page 24) 1 tsp

A pinch of asafoetida (hing) powder

Curry leaves 2 sprigs

Salt to taste

DAL WATER

200 g of tuvar dal (pigeon pea lentils)

Water 7 cups

Coriander leaves, chopped
1 heaped tsp

SEASONING

Ghee 1 tbsp

A pinch of mustard seeds

1 onion (medium-sized), chopped

METHOD

- To prepare the dal water, cook 200 g dal in 7 cups of water till soft. Allow the dal to settle (for about 30 minutes) and then take the clear water from the top.
- To make the dumplings, soak 150 g dal for an hour and then drain the water. Grind the soaked dal, chilli powder, salt and asafoetida with 3 tbsp of water.
- Add the grated coconut, onion and oil to the dal paste and mix well.
- Cook the dal mixture over medium heat, stirring continuously for 3-5 minutes until it is dry and thick enough to form dumplings.

- Add coriander leaves and rice flour to the dal and coconut paste and mix well.

- Divide the batter into 40 small portions and using the palm of your hands, lightly roll into dumplings. Do not press too hard or the dumplings will become tough.

- To make the gravy, mix the tamarind water, sambar powder, asafoetida, curry leaves and salt and bring to a boil. Simmer on low heat for 5 minutes.

- Add the dal water and coriander leaves and bring to a boil.

- Slide the dumplings, one by one, into the boiling gravy. Keep the gravy on a low rolling boil while adding the dumplings. Once all the dumplings are in the gravy, reduce the heat and simmer for 20 minutes. As they cook, the dumplings will rise to the surface of the gravy.

- In another pan, heat the ghee and fry the mustard seeds and onion. Pour over the dumpling gravy. Stir well and serve with rice.

Tip: This recipe can also be made with yellow (husked) moong dal or chana dal (husked Bengal gram).

Use the leftover 1 cup of cooked dal as follows – Add 2 green chillies, ¼ tsp turmeric, 1 tsp cumin powder and salt to the dal and cook for 10 minutes. Add two cups of any chopped greens (spinach, chawli or amaranthus, radish greens) to the dal and cook for 5 more minutes. Add the juice of half a lime and a tsp of ghee to finish. Serve hot.

Masoor Dal with Potatoes

Serves 4

INGREDIENTS

Lal masoor dal (split red lentils) ½ cup

Mild green chillies, slit length-wise 1-8 (optional)

A pinch of fresh grated ginger

Garlic cloves, crushed 3

Tomatoes (medium size), chopped 2

Potatoes, boiled, cool and cut into cubes 2

Coconut, grated 2 tbsp

A pinch of sugar

Salt to taste

SEASONING

Ghee or vegetable oil 2 tsp

A pinch of mustard seeds

Onion (large), finely-chopped 1

Garam Masala Powder 1 (Pg 23) 1 tsp

METHOD

- Wash the dal. In a saucepan, bring 3 cups of water to boil and add the dal along with green chillies, ginger and garlic. Cook for about 25 minutes till done.
- Add the tomato, potatoes, coconut, sugar and salt to the dal.
- In a small pan, heat the oil, pop the mustard seeds, fry the onion and garam masala.
- Add the seasoning to the dal, bring to a boil and simmer for 5 minutes. Serve with steamed rice or chapatis.

Rasam

Serves 4

INGREDIENTS

ORANGE PEEL MIXTURE

Fresh orange peel, chopped into tiny pieces ⅓ piece

A big pinch of asafoetida (hing) powder

Tamarind pulp ¾-inch ball soaked in 30 ml warm water

Black pepper powder ½ tsp

Butter 1 tbsp

A pinch of sugar

Salt to taste

Water 1½ ltrs

Tuvar dal (pigeon pea lentils) 125 g

Green chillies, slit 3-8

A pinch of turmeric powder

SEASONING

Ghee ½ tsp

A pinch of mustard seeds

Curry leaves 1 sprig

METHOD

- Wash the dal. Bring the water to a boil with the chillies and turmeric powder, then add the dal to it and cook till soft for about 20-25 minutes. Stir well and let the dal settle at the bottom of the pan.

- Scoop 3 cups of the clear water from the top of the dal and pour over the orange peel mixture.

- Heat the ghee in a vagharia or small pan. When hot, fry the mustard seeds till they pop and add the curry leaves. When they splutter pour the seasoning onto the orange peel dal water mixture. Bring to a boil and simmer for 10 minutes. Serve hot with rice or chapatis.

Gooseberry Drink (Amla Kadi)

Serves 4

INGREDIENTS

Amla, or salted star gooseberries, deseed 12

¼ coconut, grated

Dried red chillies, roasted 3

½-inch ball of tamarind or tamarind pulp ¼ tsp

Water 1½ cups

SEASONING

Vegetable oil 2 tsp

A pinch of mustard seeds

Small pod of garlic, skinned and crushed 1

A big pinch of asafoetida (hing) powder

Salt if necessary

METHOD

- Grind the amla, coconut, chillies and tamarind into a smooth paste. Add the water to make the paste into pouring consistency.
- Heat the oil and fry the mustard seeds and garlic. Add the asafoetida and stir before pouring the seasoning over the masala paste. Add salt and bring to a boil. Remove from heat and serve hot.

Tip: Omit tamarind in the masala and add ½ cup of sweet buttermilk to the finished kadi when cool.

Buttermilk Soup (Thaak Kadi)

Serves 4

INGREDIENTS

Sour buttermilk 1 cup

Salt to taste

Tomato (small), chopped 1

SEASONING

Vegetable oil 2 tsp

A pinch of mustard seeds

A pinch of cumin seeds

Garlic cloves, crushed 6 (optional)

Green chillies, slit 3

A big pinch of asafoetida (hing) powder

A pinch of turmeric powder

Water ¾ cup

METHOD

- Heat the oil and sauté all the seasoning ingredients.
- Add the chopped tomato and stir. Cover and cook over a low fire till soft.
- Add the water and bring it to a boil. Remove from the heat and allow it to cool. Now add the buttermilk and salt. Stir well and serve.

Tip: Add 2 tsp of besan (bengal gram flour) to the seasoning ingredients after the turmeric and mix well, cooking for 2 minutes, stirring continuously, before adding the tomato bits. Carry on as above.

If you plan to serve this a few hours after preparing it, add the buttermilk and bring the mixture to a boil. This will prevent it from souring too much. The buttermilk may curdle, but will taste just as good.

Onion in a Coconut Sauce (Onion Thambli)

Serves 2

INGREDIENTS

Onion (medium-sized), minced 1

MASALA

¼ coconut, grated

Dry red chillies, roasted 3

Tamarind pulp ¼ tsp

Sour curd or buttermilk 1¼ cups

Salt to taste

METHOD

- Grind the coconut, chillies and tamarind pulp in a mixer. Add the buttermilk to make a smooth paste.
- Add the minced onion to the masala paste in the mixer and grind on a pulse setting a few times. Add salt and serve.

Tip: Easy to prepare and often uncooked, many thamblis are made from ground leaves or vegetables and are popular in Mangalore and coastal Karnataka.

In this recipe, you can use a piece of ginger instead of onion and add a teaspoon of roasted cumin seeds to the masala.

Served cold with hot rice and a bendhi, this chutney-like sauce has a cooling effect.

Curry Leaf in Coconut & Buttermilk (Karbeva Thambli)

Serves 2

INGREDIENTS

Curry leaves 3 sprigs

Half coconut, grated

Dried red Byedgi chillies, roasted 2

Tamarind pulp ¼ tsp

Sour buttermilk 1½ cups

Salt to taste

METHOD

- Roast the curry leaves with the grated coconut till light brown. Stir continuously to prevent charring. Do not roast the curry leaves separately as they will burn easily and become bitter in taste.
- Add the chillies and tamarind, and grind to a smooth paste in a mixer. Add the buttermilk and pulse till well blended.
- Add salt to taste and serve cold with hot rice.

Tip: A seasoning of ¼ tsp of mustard seeds, ¼ tsp cumin seeds and a broken dry chilli sautéed in ¼ tsp ghee can be added at the end before serving.

You can also use an equivalent amount of *Centella asiatica* (Brahmi), fenugreek or coriander leaves instead of the curry leaves. All of them have medicinal properties.

A cooling, mildly-spiced curry served with hot rice.

Green Banana in a Coconut Sauce (Plantain Ambat)

Serves 4

INGREDIENTS

1 large (or 100 g) unripe cooking banana, or a Malabar banana, gherkins or cucumber

A pinch of turmeric powder

A pinch of asafoetida (hing) powder

Jaggery ½ tsp (optional)

Water 300 ml

Cashews 4

Chana dal (husked Bengal gram) 2 tbsp

Salt to taste

MASALA

One-fourth coconut, grated

Dry red chillies, roasted 2

Water ½ cup

SEASONING

Vegetable oil 2 tsp

A big pinch of mustard seeds

Curry leaves 1 sprig

METHOD

- Skin and cut the banana into small cubes. Mix with the turmeric and asafoetida powder, jaggery and salt. Steam till cooked and soft.

- In another pan, bring the water to a boil and add the cashews and dal. Cook for about 30 minutes till soft and done. Add this to the cooked banana cubes.

- Grind the coconut and red chillies with the water to form a smooth paste. Add to the banana and dal mixture. Mix well and simmer for 5 minutes.

- Heat the oil and fry the mustard seeds and curry leaves. Pour over the banana mixture. Stir well and serve.

Tip: A quick way to remove the banana peel is to pressure cook it with one whistle and then skin the banana immediately. If peeling with a potato peeler, don't be too fussy about removing all the peel. It doesn't matter if a bit of peel is left before cutting.

Amaranthus Dal (Thotakoora Ambat)

Serves 4

Amaranthus (chawli) leaves and stems
2 cups

Water 500 g

Tuvar dal (pigeon pea lentils) 75 g

MASALA

Half coconut, grated

Byedgi red chillies, roasted 6

Tamarind pulp 1 tsp

Water ¼ cup

Salt to taste

SEASONING

Oil 3 tsp

Mustard seeds ½ tsp

Curry leaves 2 sprigs

METHOD

- Wash the amaranthus leaves. Drain completely in a colander. Chop the amaranthus leaves if large. Cut the stems into 2-inch lengths.

- Wash the dal. In a saucepan, bring the water to a boil and add the dal. Cook for 10 minutes till half done.

- Add the amaranthus leaves and stems to the dal and continue to boil till both dal and greens are tender.

- Grind the coconut, roasted chillies and tamarind together with water to a smooth paste. Add salt to taste.

- Add the masala paste to the dal and vegetables and bring to a boil, then simmer on low heat for a few minutes.

- Heat the oil in a small pan. Add the mustard seeds. Heat till the mustard seeds pop. Add the curry leaves, stir, and pour over the dal. Serve hot with steamed rice.

Tip: Use 6 cloves of garlic or 1 chopped onion for seasoning instead of mustard seeds and curry leaves.

You can also add dried shrimp to the dal, along with the amaranthus, for an amazing flavour.

Amaranthus grows in abundance in many areas of the Konkan. It is said the reason it grows so well in kitchen gardens is that the plant is fed with the water used to clean fish.

Meat & Poultry

Mutton Curry with Cinnamon & Coriander

Serves 2

INGREDIENTS

Boneless mutton, washed and cubed 250 g

MASALA

Vegetable oil 1 tbsp

Onion, sliced 1

Coconut, grated 5 packed tbsp

Coriander seeds, 1 tsp

Cumin seeds ½ tsp

Garlic, 2 cloves

Clove 1

Small red chillies (optional) 2-8

Water ¾ cup

SEASONING

Vegetable oil or ghee 1 tbsp

Onion, minced 1

Cinnamon, powdered ¼-inch stick

Coriander leaves, chopped 2 handfuls

Salt to taste

METHOD

- Heat the oil and fry the grated coconut till light brown. Remove the coconut from the oil and, in the same pan, fry the red chillies, clove, coriander seeds, cumin seeds, garlic and finely chopped onions till soft.

- Let the mixtures cool; then, grind the coconut and masala ingredients together till very smooth, adding the water bit by bit.

- In a pan over heat, coat the mutton pieces with the masala. Add salt and bring the mixture to a boil. Reduce heat, cover tightly, and simmer for one hour till the mutton is tender. (Add another half cup of water after 30 minutes of cooking.)

- In another pan, heat ghee and fry the onion and cinnamon powder. Pour this seasoning over the mutton.

- Add the chopped coriander, stir well and serve with chapatis or puris.

Tip: This style of mutton can be cooked in a pressure cooker as well. Combine all the ingredients to high pressure and cook for 10 minutes. Reduce pressure and remove the weight. Open the cooker and cook for a further five minutes till most of the water has evaporated and only a thick gravy is left. Season, garnish, and serve.

A thick, delicately-spiced gravy redolent with fresh coriander.

Mangalorean Pork Curry (Pork Indad)

Serves 4

INGREDIENTS

Pork, cubed 500 g

MASALA

Onions, medium 3

Garlic, peeled 1 pod

Ginger, peeled 1-inch piece

Green chillies 2

Red chilli, broken 4

Bird's eye chilli 2

Peppercorns 6

Cumin seeds ½ tsp

Cloves 4

Cinnamon 2-inch stick

Turmeric powder ½ tsp

Tamarind paste 1½ tsp

Coriander leaves, chopped 2 tbsp

Toddy vinegar 5 tbsp

Ghee or vegetable oil 2 tbsp

Potatoes, sliced 2

Onions, finely-chopped 2

Water from the boiled pork 1 cup

Palm sugar 2 tsp

Salt to taste

METHOD

- Cook the pork in 2 cups of water for an hour.
- Roast the chillies, peppercorns, cloves, cinnamon and cumin one after the other, separately, till each is light brown and gives off a slight fragrance.
- Grind all together with the chopped onion, green chillies, coriander leaves, tamarind paste, turmeric powder and vinegar to make a fine, smooth paste.
- Heat the oil and fry the pork cubes till the fat is rendered. Remove the pork pieces and fry the potato slices in the same fat. Remove the potato slices.
- Fry the chopped onion in the same fat, add the masala paste, and continue to fry for 15 minutes till the colour changes. Add half a cup of water from the cooked pork slowly while the masala is frying.
- Add the sugar and adjust the salt and vinegar to taste.
- Return the pork cubes to the curry and cook for another 10 minutes.
- Garnish with the fried potato slices and serve hot with dosas, rotis, or bread.

Tip: This curry keeps well and tastes even better after a couple of days.

This sweet-and-sour pork recipe is a Mangalorean Catholic favourite.

Mangalorean Pepper Pork (Dukra Maas)

Serves 6

INGREDIENTS

Pork belly, cubed 1 kg

Peppercorns, powdered 4 tbsp

Salt 1 tsp

Toddy vinegar 3 tbsp

Turmeric powder ¼ tsp

Onions, medium 6

Tomatoes, finely-chopped 4

Tomato purée 2 tbsp

Green chillies 6

Garlic, peeled 1 pod

Ginger 2-inch piece

Vegetable oil 2 tbsp

Salt to taste

METHOD

- Wash the pork cubes and mix with the pepper powder, salt, vinegar and turmeric. Marinate for an hour or more.

- Grind the onions, chillies, garlic and ginger into a fine paste.

- Heat oil in a heavy-bottomed pan and fry the tomatoes. Once they turn into a pulp and the oil starts to separate, add the ground masala and fry on low heat till brown. If it starts sticking, add a tablespoon of water from time to time and keep stirring.

- Now add the marinated pork and sauté for a few minutes. Add half a cup of water and bring to the boil.

- Lower heat to simmering point and cook, covered, for 45 minutes till done.

- Add the tomato puree, salt and more vinegar (to taste), and cook for a further 10 minutes. Serve hot with idlis, rotis or bread.

Tip: The vinegar can be substituted with 2 tsp of tamarind paste, and the green chillies with red.

Meat Ball Curry

Serves 4 (Makes 34 balls)

INGREDIENTS

Meat, minced 500 g

Cloves 2

Cinnamon ¼-inch stick

Water 2 cups

MASALA

Flesh from half a coconut, chopped-roughly

Onions, medium, sliced 3

Ginger, peeled 1-inch piece

Garlic, peeled 4 cloves

Coriander leaves 2 handfuls

Green chillies (optional) 2-5

Poppy seeds 3 tsp

Tuvar dal (pigeon pea lentils), roasted 1 level tbsp

SEASONING

Ghee or vegetable oil 2 tbsp

Onions, finely-chopped 2

Tomato, finely-chopped 1

Cardamom, crushed 2 pods

Curry leaves 1 sprig

Turmeric powder ¼ tsp

Chilli powder (optional) 1½ tsp

Salt to taste

METHOD

- Grind the minced meat in a blender with the cloves and cinnamon.
- Grind the coconut, poppy seeds, chillies, onions, ginger, coriander leaves, garlic and dal together to make a smooth paste. This makes about 1½ cups of masala.
- Add one-third of this masala along with the salt to the mince and mix well.
- In a pan, heat the ghee and fry the cardamom, curry leaves and onions till soft and brown. Add the turmeric and chilli powder, and give it a stir.
- Add the chopped tomato and cook till it can be mashed. Add the rest of the masala and cook till brown, stirring continuously for about 10 minutes.
- Add the water and bring to a boil. Reduce heat.
- Form small balls of the ground mince and drop into the simmering liquid one by one. Simmer gently for about half an hour till cooked. Do not stir after adding the meat balls. The gravy reduces to become quite thick. Serve hot with rice or rotis.

Garlicky Minced Meat Curry

Serves 4

INGREDIENTS

Meat, minced 500 g

Onions, finely-chopped 2

Ginger, peeled 2-inch piece

Garlic, peeled 20 cloves

Turmeric powder ½ tsp

Cumin powder ½ tsp

Chilli powder (optional) 1 tsp

SEASONING

Vegetable oil or ghee 3 tbsp

Cloves 4

Cardamom, crushed 4 pods

Cinnamon, crushed 1-inch stick

Onions, finely-chopped 2

Coriander leaves, finely-chopped 2 handfuls

Curry leaves 2 sprigs

Potatoes, peeled and cubed 250 g

Coconut, roughly chopped 1

Water ¾ cup

Lime, juiced 1

Salt to taste

METHOD

- In a bowl, mix the 2 finely-chopped onions, chilli and turmeric powder with the minced meat.
- Grind the cumin, ginger and garlic to a paste, and add to the minced meat. Set aside for 5 minutes.
- Heat the oil and fry the cloves, cardamom, cinnamon, 2 finely-chopped onions and curry leaves. Add the minced meat and chopped coriander, and cook over low heat for 10 minutes.
- Add the cubed potatoes and salt and cook for 10 minutes more till potatoes are done.
- Meanwhile, grind the coconut with the water and extract the milk (see page 18). Pour the coconut milk and lime juice into the mince mixture. Stir and cook for another 5 minutes, then serve hot.

Meat & Potatoes in a Mint & Coriander Green Curry

Serves 4

INGREDIENTS

Meat, washed and cubed 250 g

Potatoes, boiled, peeled and cubed 2

Salt ½ tsp

MASALA

Coconut, grated 1 heaped tbsp

Ginger, peeled ½-inch piece

Garlic, peeled 8 cloves

Poppy seeds 3 tsp

Turmeric powder ¼ tsp

Onion, finely-chopped 1

Green chillies (optional) 2

Black peppercorns 6

Mint leaves 18

Coriander leaves 1 handful

SEASONING

Vegetable oil 2 tbsp

Black cumin seeds 1 pinch

Cardamom, slit open 2 pods

Cloves, crushed 4

Cinnamon, crushed ½-inch stick

Onions, very finely-chopped 2

Yoghurt 4 tbsp

METHOD

- Cook the meat in 2 cups of water till tender. This takes an hour over low heat in a saucepan or 10 minutes in a pressure cooker.

- To make the masala, grind the coconut, ginger, garlic, poppy seeds, turmeric, onion, green chillies, peppercorns, mint and coriander leaves with 3 tbsp of water till smooth.

- Heat the oil and fry the black cumin, cardamom, cloves, cinnamon and onions, and pour over the ground masala.

- Cook the paste over a low flame till it browns and releases an aroma. This can take up to 10 minutes.

- Add the cooked meat, potatoes and salt, and stir over low heat, cooking for another 5 minutes. Add some water to prevent sticking, if needed.

- Take off the heat, add yoghurt and mix well. Serve hot with rice or rotis.

Chicken Dry (Kori Sukka)

Serves 4

INGREDIENTS

Chicken, cut into 2-inch pieces 1 kg

Potatoes, peeled and cubed (optional) 200 g

MARINADE

Garlic, peeled 3-4 cloves

Ginger, peeled 1-inch piece

Lemon, juiced 1

Red chilli powder 3 tsp

Turmeric powder ½ tsp

MASALA

Oil 2 tsp

Onions, sliced 2

Coconut, grated 3 tbsp

Poppy seeds 1½ tbsp

Oil 1 tbsp

Bay leaf 1

Black cardamoms 2

Cloves 4

Cinnamon, crushed 1-inch stick

Black peppercorns 8

Onion, finely chopped 1

Jaggery or sugar 1 tsp

Coriander leaves, chopped 1 handful

Salt ½ tsp

METHOD

- Skin, wash and cut the chicken into pieces.
- Boil the potato cubes till done.
- Grind the garlic and ginger along with the spices, salt, and lime juice in a blender to make a marinade.
- Add this marinade to the chicken pieces and mix till well coated. Cover and refrigerate for a couple of hours.
- Heat a little oil in a pan and fry the chopped onions till translucent. Remove.
- Roast the coconut in a non-stick frying pan over low heat till golden in colour. Remove and roast the poppy seeds separately till golden.
- Cool the coconut and poppy seeds, and grind along with the onions to make a smooth paste. Add up to 2 tsbp of water if required.

- Now heat the rest of the oil and sauté the whole spices, bay leaf, cardamom, cloves, cinnamon and peppercorns. As the aroma of spices rises, add the sliced onion and sauté till golden brown.

- Now add the marinated chicken pieces and fry till golden, turning frequently. Add the ground paste and fry, stirring often. Add a tablespoon of water from time to time to prevent sticking and continue cooking the paste for at least 5 minutes.

- Add the salt and jaggery. Cover and cook on a low flame for about 15 minutes, stirring frequently. Add the cooked potato, mix well and cook for a further 5 minutes.

- Add the chopped coriander, adjust the seasoning if required, and serve hot with rice or rotis.

Kundapur Chicken Gravy (Kori Gassi)

Serves 4

INGREDIENTS

Chicken pieces, washed 1 kg

MASALA

Coconut, grated ¾

Red Byedgi chillies, broken into bits, 2-6

Cinnamon, broken 2-inch piece

Cloves 6

Peppercorns 8

Cumin seeds 1 tsp

Coriander seeds 2 tsp

Garlic, peeled (optional) 5 cloves

Water 1 cup

Sesame oil 2 tsp

Curry leaves 2 sprigs (about 30)

Onions, finely chopped, 2

Tomatoes, chopped 2

Salt 1 tsp

METHOD

- Roast the masala ingredients one by one, separately, till light brown.
- Grind the roasted masala in a blender till smooth, adding 1 cup of water to make a fine paste.
- Heat the oil in a saucepan and fry the cumin seeds and curry leaves. As they splutter, add the chopped onion and sauté till soft and translucent.
- Add the chopped tomatoes and cook till the tomatoes become a paste and the oil separates from the mixture.
- In a separate pan, heat 12 teaspoons of oil and when smoking put in the chicken pieces. Stir over high heat till the pieces change colour. Add to the tomato-onion mixture.
- Now add the coconut masala paste and sauté, stirring constantly till the colour changes. This takes about 2 minutes. Add ¼ cup of water and the salt and cover tightly.
- Cook for 25 minutes till the chicken is done. Serve hot with rice.

Seafood

Tamarind Fish Curry (Kane Ghashi)

Serves 4

INGREDIENTS

Lady fish, cut into large cubes 500 g

MASALA

Half a coconut, roughly chopped

Red chillies, roasted 4

Tamarind ¾ inch-sized ball

Water 1 cup

Coriander leaves, chopped 1 cup

Green chillies, minced 2

Ginger, finely-grated ½ tsp

Onion (medium-sized), finely-chopped 1

Coconut oil 1 tbsp

Salt to taste

METHOD

- Grind the coconut, red chillies and tamarind into a smooth paste with the water in a blender.

- Combine the coriander, chillies, ginger, onion, coconut oil and salt and add to the masala.

- In a pan over medium heat, bring this mixture to a boil.

- Gently add the cubed fish and simmer for 15 minutes till done. Do not stir the curry, just shake the pan to mix. Serve hot with rice.

Tip: You can omit the green coriander, green chillies, onion and ginger and A. Fry 1 tsp coriander seeds and 6 fenugreek seeds in a teaspoon of oil. Add these spices to the coconut while grinding. B. Fry ¼ teaspoon of asafoetida (hing) in a teaspoon of oil. Add to coconut while grinding.

Clams in a Dry Hot Coconut Masala (Khubbe Sukke)

Serves 6

INGREDIENTS

Clams 1 kg (about 100)

Coconut oil 2 tbsp

Onions (large), finely-chopped 2

Turmeric powder ½ tsp

Coriander powder 2 tsp

Black peppercorns, ground 10

Byedgi chillies, roasted 10

Garam masala powder 1 tsp (see page 23)

Coconut, grated 1 cup

Tamarind paste 1 tsp

Fresh coriander, chopped ½ cup

Sea salt ½ tsp

METHOD

- Soak the clams in a large pan of water till all the sand on the shells is washed away. Discard any clams that have opened.

- Make a paste of all the powdered spices, coconut and tamarind.

- Heat the oil, pop the mustard seeds and fry the curry leaves.

- Add the onions and fry till pale brown.

- Add the ground masala paste and fry well for 10-15 minutes till it no longer tastes of raw spice.

- Add clams and mix well till coated with the masala. Cover and cook for 10 minutes. The clams will sweat, and the shells will crack, but cook till most of the water has dried up. Again, discard any clams that have not opened.

- Add the chopped coriander and mix well. Check for saltiness before adding any more salt. Serve with rice and dalithoi (see page 75).

Tip: When buying clams, check that they are tightly shut. Remove any that are damaged or cracked. If any clams remain unopened after cooking remove them as well.

Ginger Garlic Fried Fish

Serves 4-6

INGREDIENTS

1-inch thick slices of fish 500 g

MASALA

Ginger 2-inch piece

Garlic cloves 20

Turmeric powder 1 tsp

Red chilli powder 2 tsp

Fresh coriander, chopped 2 cups

Salt to taste

Egg whites, whisked 2

Breadcrumbs 4 tbsp

Vegetable oil for deep frying

METHOD

- Grind the masala ingredients together to make a smooth paste. Do not add any water.
- Pat the fish slices dry and coat with the masala paste on both sides. Marinate in the refrigerator for 4 hours.
- Heat the oil on a medium fire. Dip each fish slice in the egg white, roll in the breadcrumbs and fry in the hot oil till done, turning over once or twice. You can fry 1 to 2 slices at a time. Serve hot.

Prawns in Coconut Curry (Sungta Ambat)

Serves 4

INGREDIENTS

MASALA

Coconut oil 2 tbsp

Onions, chopped 1½ cup

Garlic cloves 10 small or 5 large

Coconut, grated 1 cup

Coriander seeds, roasted 1 tbsp

Dry red chillies 6

Tamarind paste ½ tsp

Turmeric powder ½ tsp

Coconut oil 1 tsp

Large prawns 750 g

Green chilli, chopped 1

Kokum (optional) 2 pieces

Salt to taste

METHOD

- Heat the oil and fry the chopped onions till golden brown. Add the garlic cloves and fry for 2 minutes more.

- Roast the grated coconut in a non-stick frying pan over very low heat to prevent burning. When pale brown, remove and roast the coriander seeds.

- Grind the coconut, onions, garlic, coriander seeds, red chillies, tamarind and turmeric powder in a blender with a quarter cup of water to make a smooth paste.

- Heat the coconut oil and fry the green chillies. Add the masala paste and sauté for 5-7 minutes. Add a little water if the masala paste sticks to the pan and continue to sauté till the mixture browns, signaling its cooked.

- Add the water and kokum, if using, to make a thick curry. Bring to a boil.

- Now add the prawns and simmer till they turn pink in colour. Add salt to taste. Serve hot with rice or roti.

Mustard Fish Curry

Makes 4 to 6 servings

INGREDIENTS

1-inch thick slices of fish 500 g

Turmeric ½ tsp

Powdered sea salt ½ tsp

MASALA

Mustard seeds 2 heaped tbsp

Green chillies, 6

Turmeric powder ½ tsp

Juice of 1 lime

Water 6 tbsp

Vegetable oil or clarified butter/ghee 4 tbsp

Green chillies, slit length-wise 6

Salt to taste

Water ¼ cup

METHOD

- Wash the fish slices and pat dry. Mix the turmeric and salt and sprinkle on both sides of the fish slices.
- Grind the mustard seeds, green chillies, turmeric and lime juice into a smooth paste with the water.
- Heat the oil to smoking point in a frying pan and fry one slice of fish at a time for about 2 minutes on each side till the colour changes from pink to white. Remove from oil.
- In the same hot oil, drop the green chillies and stir for a minute. Add the mustard paste and fry, stirring continuously till it turns light brown.
- Add the salt and water and bring to a boil.
- Slide the fried fish slices back into the curry and simmer till cooked, turning over gently once or twice. Serve with rice or chapatis.

Tip: Reduce the number of green chillies if you prefer a milder curry.

Easy Fried Fish

Serves 4-6

INGREDIENTS

Fish, cut into large, thick slices 500 g

MASALA

Red chillies, roasted 6

Coriander seeds 1 heaped tsp

Rice 2 heaped tsp

Asafoetida (hing) powder ¼ tsp

Salt to taste

Water 2 tbsp

Oil for shallow frying

METHOD

- Grind the chillies, coriander seeds, rice, asafoetida and salt together with the water to make a smooth paste.
- Rub the fish slices with a little salt and let it stand for 5 minutes. Wash and drain the fish well.
- Smear the fish slices with the masala paste and set aside for 10 minutes.
- Heat the oil in a thick pan over medium heat. Fry the slices for about 10 minutes till cooked, turning over gently once or twice in between. Serve with chapatis or rice.

Tip: Any salt or freshwater fish will work for this recipe. If you are using Malabar Sole, make the pieces into large fillets.

Chilli Tamarind Dried Prawns (Sukkale Sungta Phanna Upkari)

Serves 4-6 as a side dish

INGREDIENTS

Dried or fresh prawns 2 cups

A pinch of turmeric

Coconut oil 2 tbsp

Onions (large), finely-chopped 3

Tamarind paste 1 tsp

Red chilli powder (made from Byedgi chillies) ½ tbsp (or to your taste)

Coconut, grated (optional) 2 tbsp

Salt to taste

Water ½ cup

METHOD

- For dried prawns, clean the prawns, remove heads and tails and soak in water with a pinch of turmeric for 10 minutes. Wash under running water to remove any sand. For fresh prawns, wash and remove heads and tails, then set aside. Keep a few prawns with tails.

- Heat the oil and fry the chopped onions till they are brown. Do not burn. If you're using dried prawns, add them now and allow them to cook for 3-4 minutes until they change colour.

- Add the chilli powder and coconut, if using, and fry.

- Add the tamarind paste, salt and water. Bring to a simmer and cook for 10 minutes. If you are using fresh prawns, add them at this stage and sauté for about 3-4 minutes until they change colour.

- The prawns should be coated with a thick sauce. Serve with plain rice.

A very hot sweet-sour preparation.

Shark Curry (Mori Randayi)

Serves 4-6

INGREDIENTS

Indian Dog Shark or Mori, skinned and cut into 1½-inch cubes 750 g

Turmeric powder 1 tsp

Salt 1 tsp

Ginger, grated 3-inch piece

Garlic cloves 8

Coriander powder 1½ tbsp

Red chilli powder 2 tsp

Sesame oil 4 tbsp

Onions, chopped 2 cup

Asafoetida (hing) powder ¼ tsp

MASALA

Sesame seeds 1 tbsp

Coriander seeds 2 tbsp

Coconut, grated 1 cup

Garam masala 1 tbsp (see page 23)

METHOD

- Rub turmeric powder and salt on the shark cubes and set aside.
- Make a paste by grinding the ginger, garlic, coriander powder and chilli powder. Marinate the fish in this paste by coating it gently.
- Dry roast the spices separately in a non-stick frying pan over a low flame. Start with the sesame and coriander seeds. Remove, then gently roast the grated coconut. Do not burn.
- Grind the coconut, sesame and coriander along with the garam masala.
- Heat the sesame oil and fry the chopped onions. Add the asafoetida and sauté for another minute.
- Add the marinated fish cubes and fry for a few minutes, turning gently from time to time.
- Add the ground masala and a cup of water, cover and cook for about 5 minutes till the fish changes colour and is done. Garnish with chopped fresh coriander and serve hot with plain rice.

Crab in a Coconut Gravy (Kurle Ambat)

Serves 4

INGREDIENTS

Medium-sized black river crabs 6

Vegetable oil 2 tbsp

Onions (large), finely-chopped 2

MASALA

Vegetable oil 2 tsp

Coriander seeds 3 tbsp

Mustard seeds ⅓ tsp

Fenugreek seeds 1 tsp

Byedgi chillies 10

Turmeric powder ½ tsp

1-inch ball of tamarind or tamarind paste ½ tsp

Coconut, grated 1

Salt to taste

METHOD

- Wash and clean the crabs. Lightly crush the legs.
- Heat the oil and fry the spices separately, one by one, in a heavy-bottomed pan taking care not to burn them.
- Grind the fried spices with the turmeric powder, coconut and tamarind to a smooth paste.
- Heat the remaining oil and fry the onions till golden brown.
- Add the ground masala and salt. Cook for 8 minutes stirring frequently. Add a little water from time to time if the masala sticks to the pan. Add a cup of water to the cooked masala and bring to a boil.
- Add the crabs and cook for around 10 minutes, till coated with the masala. Serve hot with rice. (This curry tastes even better after standing for a few hours.)

Tip: River crabs can be substituted with sea crabs which are often sweeter. Have the fishmonger clean and crack the crabs and cook within an hour or two of buying.

Rice & Breads

Jack Seed Dosa (Soornali Dosa)

Makes 6 dosas

INGREDIENTS

Jackfruit seeds 12

Rice, washed 125 g

Urad dal (husked black gram),
washed 1 tsp

Water 1½ cups

Coconut, grated 3 heaped tbsp

Jaggery 1-inch ball

Salt to taste

Ghee for frying

METHOD

- Steam or boil the jackfruit seeds till soft. Skin.

- Soak the rice and dal in water for 3 hours. Drain and reserve the water.

- In a mixer, grind the rice, dal, coconut and jackfruit seeds to make a smooth paste. Add the reserved water during this process.

- Combine the jaggery and salt in a bowl and pour the jackfruit and rice mixture over it. Cover and keep overnight.

- On the next day, add water if necessary to loosen the mixture and make a batter that can be ladled.

- Heat a non-stick frying pan or a tava. Brush the surface with a teaspoon of oil and pour in a ladleful of the batter. Tilt the pan to spread the batter. Cover and cook for 2 minutes. Brush some ghee over the top and turn the dosa. Cook for 1-2 minutes to make it crisp. Serve hot.

Curry Leaf Dosa (Karbeva Polo)

Makes 9 dosas

INGREDIENTS

Tuvar dal (pigeon pea lentils) 2 tbsp

Rice 6 tbsp

Three-fourth of a coconut

Green chillies 3-6

Curry leaves 1½ cups

Water ½ cup

Salt ½ tsp (or to taste)

Vegetable oil 6 tbsp

METHOD

- Soak the rice and lentils together in hot water for 30 minutes. Drain.
- Grind the coconut, chillies and curry leaves together to make a coarse paste. Add the soaked rice and lentils and grind again with half a cup water to make a thick paste with the consistency of semolina. Add the rest of the water and salt. Let the mixture stand overnight for about 16 hours.
- Divide the paste into 9 portions.
- Heat a non-stick frying pan or tava and brush it with a teaspoon of oil.
- Ladle one portion of the paste on the frying pan and spread to a 5-6-inch diameter circle. Cook over low heat till light brown. Put a little oil around the edges and surface of the polo before turning. Cook on the other side till light brown. This takes some time as the dosa can break if cooked too fast. Cook the rest, and serve hot with chutney or pickle.

Onion & Cabbage Mini Dosa (Sanna Polo)

Makes 9 dosas

INGREDIENTS

Raw rice ½ cup

Yellow moong dal (husked moong) ½ cup

Coconut, grated ⅓ cup

Byedgi chillies, roasted 3-5

Tamarind paste ½ tsp

Onions, chopped ½ cup

Cabbage, chopped ½ cup

Salt ½ tsp

Vegetable oil for frying 4 tbsp

A pinch of asafoetida (hing) powder

METHOD

- Soak the rice and dal together for an hour. Drain. Make a paste of the rice, dal, coconut, red chillies and tamarind without adding water.
- Add the asafoetida, salt, chopped onion and cabbage to the paste and mix well.
- Brush 2 teaspoons of oil on a non-stick frying pan or tava and heat. Oil your hands and take a large tablespoon of the mixture. Flatten into a patty on the palms of your hands and then slap on to the heated frying pan. Use your fingers to flatten the patty further till it is about 3-inch in diameter and ¼-inch thick. About 3 should fit in a 10-inch deep pan. Cover and cook for 2 minutes.
- Add a teaspoon of oil around and on the dosas. Turn, and fry the other side for another 2 minutes till evenly browned. Repeat till all the dosas are done. Serve hot or cold with tamarind sauce, or any chutney.

Tip: This batter can also be steamed in greased idli cups for 25 minutes (Sanno Khotto) or deep fried in small 1½-inch balls to make vadas (Cabbage Ambodos).

Mixed Flour Dosa

Makes 8 large dosas

INGREDIENTS

Whole-wheat flour 250 g

Half a coconut

Green chillies 2-4

Water 1 cup

Coriander leaves, chopped 1 tbsp

A big pinch asafoetida (hing) powder

Salt ½ tsp

SEASONING

Ghee or vegetable oil 3 tsp

Mustard seeds ⅓ tsp

Curry leaves 1 sprig

Buttermilk ½ cup

Water, ½ cup or as required

METHOD

- Grind the coconut and chillies in a mixer till very fine. Add the wheat flour and grind for at least 5 minutes, slowly adding a cup of water till a smooth batter is formed.

- Add the coriander leaves, asafoetida and salt to the batter.

- Heat the oil and fry the mustard seeds and curry leaves. Pour this seasoning over the batter.

- Add the buttermilk to the batter and mix well. You can add up to half a cup water to make a thin batter that pours freely from the ladle.

- Heat a non-stick frying pan or tava over medium heat. Pour 2 teaspoons of oil in the pan and turn to coat the surface with oil. When the oil reaches smoking point, pour in 2 ladles of the batter and spread as thinly as possible. Cover and cook for 2 minutes.

- Brush the exposed surface of the dosa with ½ tsp oil and turn. Cook uncovered for 2 minutes more. Remove from pan.

- Repeat the above to make 7 more 9-inch dosas. Serve hot with chutneys, chutney powders or any vegetable or dal.

Tip: Substitute the coriander leaves and asafoetida with 1 tsp grated ginger and 2 tsp minced onion. Add ½ tsp of cumin to the seasoning.

Cucumber Dosa (Thousali)

Makes 6 dosas

INGREDIENTS

Idli rice, or any other short grain rice
1 cup

Thin, beaten rice 2 heaped tbsp

Water 2¼ cups

Cucumber, grated 1 cup

Baking soda 1 tsp

Coconut, grated 1 lightly-packed cup

Ghee or vegetable oil

METHOD

- Wash both types of rice and soak in the water for 6-8 hours before use. Drain the rice and reserve the water.
- Grind into a coarse paste with the coconut, adding the reserved water.
- Mix the cucumber, cucumber juice, soda and salt with the ground paste. Add water, if required, to make a batter of pouring consistency.
- Heat a non-stick frying pan with a tablespoon of oil to smoking point. Pour a large ladleful of batter and tilt the pan to spread evenly. Cover and cook for 2 minutes till the dosa is crisp on one side and craters have appeared in the dosa. Cook till golden brown on the lower side. Remove and serve hot with pickle, chutney or honey.

Tip: Green cucumbers, available in the Konkan during the monsoons around Ganesh Chaturthi, are often used in this recipe. You can add 2 tablespoons of grated jaggery to the mixture when grinding the rice to make a sweet Thousali.

Banana Dosa (Kel Dosa)

Makes 8-10 dosas

INGREDIENTS

Flour (maida) ⅓ cup

Rice flour ⅓ cup

Water 1 cup

Yoghurt ⅓ cup

Half a coconut, roughly-chopped

Water ¼ cup

Salt 1 tsp

A big pinch of baking soda

Ripe bananas, finely-chopped 2

Ghee or oil for frying

METHOD

- Mix the flours together. Gradually add water, mixing slowly till it is smooth and free of lumps. Now, add the yoghurt and mix again. Cover and let this mixture stand for 8 hours.

- Grind the coconut in a blender and add the flour mixture. Grind for about 2 minutes adding ¼ cup of water to the mixture.

- Add salt, baking soda and banana pieces to the batter and mix thoroughly. The batter should be of a pouring consistency.

- Brush a teaspoon or two of oil on a non-stick frying pan. Bring it to smoking point and pour 2 ladlefuls of the batter, tilting the pan to let the batter spread. Cover and cook for 2 minutes till the underside of the dosa is brown and crisp. There is no need to turn these over unless you prefer crisper dosas. Serve with chutneys or Lentil Chutney Powder/Parpu Podi (page 159).

Savoury Semolina Cakes with Yoghurt (Curd Idli)

Makes 16 idlis

INGREDIENTS

Fine semolina (rava) 250 g

Yoghurt 2 cups

Coconut, grated 6 tbsp

Asafoetida (hing) powder ¼ tsp

Baking soda ¼ tsp

Cashewnuts, broken into bits
(optional) 10

Salt to taste

Water ½-¾ cup

SEASONING

Ghee 4 tbsp

Mustard seeds ½ tsp

Green chillies, slit, deseeded and
chopped 2

Curry leaves 2 sprigs

METHOD

- Heat the ghee and fry mustard seeds, chillies and curry leaves. Add the semolina and roast over low heat, stirring continuously till very pale, light brown. (Do not brown further or the idlis will turn out dry.) Take the pan off the heat and let the semolina cool.

- Mix the yoghurt, coconut, asafoetida, nuts and soda together. When the semolina has cooled, add it to the yogurt and mix well. Add a little water if required, should the consistency be too thick. You can let this mixture stand to ferment for an hour or cook immediately.

- Spoon into greased idli cups and steam for 15-20 minutes.

Tip: This batter makes 'instant' idlis as there is no need to soak the mix overnight. The semolina can be seasoned and roasted a day before and mixed with the curds just before cooking to save time. It makes a filling breakfast.

Moong Dal & Ginger Idli

Makes 6 idlis

INGREDIENTS

Whole moong dal (husked green gram) 65 g

Coconut, grated 2 tbsp

Tamarind paste ¼ tsp

Mild green chillies 2

Dry red chilli, roasted 1

A big pinch of grated ginger

Water ⅓ cup

Salt to taste

- Wash and soak the dal for an hour. Drain.
- Grind all the ingredients together in a mixer to make a fine paste to the consistency of fine semolina.
- Add ⅓ cup water and pulse a few times to mix well.
- Fill six generously greased idli cups with this mixture. Do not fill more than three-quarters full.
- Steam till cooked for about 25-30 minutes. Do not overcook or the idlis will dry out. Serve with ghee.

Tip: You can pour the whole batter into greased bowl or pan and steam till cooked. Cut the cake into cubes and serve.

Horse Gram Idli (Kulitha Idli)

Makes 24-26 idlis

INGREDIENTS

Horse gram (kulith) dal 50 g

Whole urad dal (husked black gram) 50 g

Water 1 cup

Semolina (rava) 150 g

Water 10 cups

Ginger ½ tsp

Green chillies, minced 2-6

Salt to taste

METHOD

- Wash the dals and soak together in water for 4-5 hours. Drain and reserve the water. Keep the reserved water refrigerated so that it is ice cold for use later.

- Pour the semolina into 10 cups of water and stir for a minute. Let the semolina settle. Decant and discard the water from the top.

- Grind the soaked dals without any water to begin with. Slowly add a bit of the reserved ice cold water and pulse for a few seconds at a time. Continue adding a part of the reserved water and pulsing for a few seconds till the paste is very smooth and fluffy. Do not grind continuously as this heats the batter and prevents it from rising properly after. Do not add too much water or make the batter runny.

- Combine the ground dal with the semolina and mix well. Let it stand overnight for 8 hours or more.

- Add the ginger, minced chillies and salt. Mix well.

- Spoon into greased idli cups till two-thirds full. Now, steam till cooked for about 15 minutes till done. Steaming can be done in a pressure cooker without the weight on. When the pressure has built up and steam comes through the spout, cover it with an inverted steel cup. Time 15 minutes after reaching full pressure. Test for readiness by inserting a fork or stick into the centre of an idli. If it comes out, clean the idlis are done. Serve with ghee, chutney or fresh pickle.

Tip: This is a tasty, nutty steamed cake which is very healthy. For variation, add ½ tsp of soaked fenugreek seeds to the dals when grinding. Prep 20 hours ahead of time.

Brown Cow Peas Idli (Bagade Idli)

Makes 15-16 idlis

INGREDIENTS

Brown cow peas
(red lobhia/chawli) 125 g

Whole urad dal
(husked black gram) 65 g

Green chillies, minced 2

A big pinch of asafoetida (hing) powder

Salt to taste

METHOD

- Soak the washed dals together in 250 ml water for 4 hours. Drain and reserve the water.

- Grind the dals together for a few minutes in a mixer with part of the water. Try to aerate the mixture as much as possible. Begin by pulsing a few times, then remove the top of the blender and grind the mixture sporadically. Rest every few seconds. Add enough of the water to the ground paste for it to reach a pouring consistency. At the same time, the mixture should not be too smooth or sticky. It should have a gritty texture. Check that the batter coats the back of a ladle thickly. Pour into a large pot. Do not mix. Cover and let it stand overnight.

- In the morning add the minced chilli, asafoetida and salt. Stir and then beat with a whisk for a minute or two to add as much air as possible to the batter.

- Grease the idli cups and fill each cup till half full.

- Put the trivet at the bottom of the pressure cooker and fill with an inch of water. Place idli stand on top of trivet and fasten the cooker lid. Do **not** put the weight on. Bring to a boil on high heat. When steam begins to appear from the cooker spout, reduce heat to minimum and steam for about 7 minutes.

- Remove the cooker from flame. Do not open. Let it cool for 5-10 minutes. Open the cooker, remove the idli stand and place horizontally on the kitchen platform for the water to drain. Loosen the idlis with a knife to demould and serve hot with chutneys or ghee.

Tip: The idlis can be made in steamer instead of a pressure cooker. Bring the water in the steamer to a boil and as steam rises, pour the batter into the idli cups. Place the idli cups in the top half of the steamer pan and steam for 12 minutes till done.

Banana Flatbread (Kel Paratha)

Makes 8

INGREDIENTS

Ripe banana (medium-sized), mashed 1

Butter, melted 2 tbsp

A pinch of asafoetida (hing) powder

Rice flour 3 tsp

Bengal gram (chana) flour 3 tsp

White flour (maida) 3 tsp

Semolina (rava) ½ cup

Sugar 1 tsp

Whole wheat flour ½ cup

Half a coconut, finely grated

Green chillies crushed in 1 tablespoon water. Strain, remove skins and reserve the chilli water 4 (optional)

Water 1-2 tbsp

Vegetable oil for frying 3 tbsp

METHOD

- Mix all the ingredients in a bowl and add enough water, bit by bit, to make a firm dough. If you don't add the green chilli water, add just 2 tbsp of water to make the dough. If using the chilli water, reduce the amount of water added. Knead the dough for 10 minutes, cover and set aside for half an hour.

- Divide dough into 8 equal portions. Form 3-inch patties using the palms of your hands. Dust with wheat flour, and roll out into 9-inch diameter circles.

- Heat a non-stick frying pan to smoking point, brush with a teaspoon of oil and cook the paratha. Cook for a minute or two till you see brown spots on the underside, then turn the paratha over. Cook on the other side for another 2 minutes. You can add another teaspoon of oil to the pan while the paratha is cooking. When it is golden brown, it is done.

Lemon Coconut Rice (Chithranna)

Serves 5

INGREDIENTS

Rice, cooked 250 g (you can use leftover boiled rice)

One-fourth a coconut, grated

A pinch of turmeric powder

Juice of 1 lime

Salt 1 tsp

MASALA

Black peppercorns 25-30

Sesame seeds 1 heaped tbsp

Whole urad dal (husked black gram) 1 heaped tbsp

Chana dal (husked Bengal gram) 1 heaped tbsp

SEASONING

Ghee or oil 25-50 g

A pinch of mustard seeds

A pinch of cumin seeds

Green chillies, slit 2-8 (or as per taste)

METHOD

- Mix the cooked rice, grated coconut, turmeric, salt and lime juice and set aside.
- Roast the peppercorns, sesame seeds, and dals separately till light brown in colour. Mix together and grind into a powder.
- Combine the masala powder and the rice mixture.
- Heat the ghee or oil and fry the mustard and cumin seeds as well as the green chillies. Pour this seasoning over the rice and cook for 10 minutes over low to medium heat. Serve hot.

Note: If you reduce the amount of ghee and oil in the seasoning, add a couple of tablespoons of water to the rice at the end before cooking for 10 minutes.

Popular in the Karnataka area of the Konkan region, this lemon rice recipe has many variations. You can omit the lime juice and add one-third of a grated raw mango to the coconut. Grind the two to make a chutney to be added at the end, after seasoning the rice. This version of the recipe is known as Mavinkai Chitranna. Garnishes include chopped green coriander and roasted peanuts.

Sweet Semolina Flat bread (Soji Paratha)

Makes 8

INGREDIENTS

Fine semolina (rava) 4 heaped tbsp

Wheat flour 1½ tbsp

Buttermilk 8 tbsp

Butter 2 tbsp

Jaggery, grated 3 tsp (or sugar 2 tsp)

Coconut, grated 2 tbsp

Salt to taste

Ghee for frying

METHOD

- Mix the semolina, wheat flour, buttermilk and butter.
- Combine the coconut and sugar together along with the salt and crush.
- Mix the semolina and coconut mixtures together.
- Divide into 8 equal portions. Flatten each portion into a ⅛-inch thick circle on a piece of greaseproof paper.
- Heat a non-stick frying pan over low heat. Add a teaspoon of ghee. Cook the paratha on the hot pan for 3-5 minutes. Add a teaspoon of ghee on the surface of the paratha and then turn over gently. Cook for another 3 minutes till golden brown, turning over once or twice. Serve hot.

Five Flour Biscuit Puri

Makes 20

INGREDIENTS

Wheat flour ¼ cup

White flour (maida) ¼ cup

Rice flour 2 tbsp

Gram flour (besan) 2 tbsp

A pinch of asafoetida (hing) powder

Green chillies, minced 1-4

Coconut, grated 4 tbsp

Semolina (rava) ¼ cup

Curry leaves, finely-chopped 2 sprigs

Salt to taste

METHOD

- Mix all the flours, salt and asafoetida.

- Crush the chillies and grated coconut with a mortar and pestle. Add this to the flours and crumble to make a mixture.

- Add just enough water to gather these ingredients together to make a ball and knead together for 4 minutes till smooth.

- Sprinkle the semolina and chopped curry leaves over the ball of dough and continue to knead for a minute. Cover and set aside for half an hour.

- Now, divide the dough into 16 equal parts and roll each into a ball. Roll out to 4-inch diameter circles on a floured surface.

- Heat 1 cup of vegetable oil till smoking point and fry the puris one by one, pressing gently on the side of each one as it is immersed in the hot oil. This makes them puff. When golden brown, remove and drain on kitchen towels. The puri should be crisp and flaky. Reheat the oil till smoking point after every batch of four. Serve hot with chutneys or curries.

Potato Pulao (Batat Bhath)

Serves 5

INGREDIENTS

Rice, cooked 250 g

One-fourth of a fresh coconut, grated

Garam Masala Powder 2 (page 23) 2 tsp

Potatoes (medium-sized), boiled, cooled
and cut into cubes 8

Juice of 1 lime

Salt to taste

SEASONING

Ghee or oil 3 tbsp

A pinch of mustard seeds

Onions (medium-sized), finely-chopped 4

Green chillies, slit length-wise 3-8

METHOD

- Mix the cooked rice, coconut, garam masala powder, lime juice and salt.
- Heat the ghee and fry the mustard seeds, onions and chillies. Pour this over the cubed potatoes and cook over a medium flame stirring constantly.
- Add the rice mixture and reduce heat. Cook for 10 minutes stirring frequently. Serve hot.

Tip: Add a cup of cooked green peas and reduce the quantity of potatoes by half.

Snacks & Savouries

Arrowroot Murku (Kuvya Peet Murku)

Makes 8 pieces

INGREDIENTS

Arrowroot (ararot) 1 cup

Whole urad dal (husked black gram), roasted over a low heat till light brown ½ cup

Rice flour ¼ cup

Butter 2 tbsp

Red chilli powder 1 level tsp

Salt to taste

Cumin ½ tsp

Oil for deep-frying

METHOD

- Make a smooth powder of the arrowroot, if it is lumpy, and then tie in a piece of thick cloth and steam for 15 minutes.
- Wash the whole urad dal and soak it in 1 cup of water for an hour. Grind into a paste using the same water.
- Combine the paste, arrowroot powder and the rest of the ingredients except the cumin and oil. Grind again for a few more minutes.
- Use the dal mixture to make a dough. Add cumin and knead well.
- To make the murku, press the dough through a murku mould on a piece of greaseproof paper into 2 or 3 concentric circles of about 2-3 inches in diameter.
- In a deep-bottomed pan, heat the oil to smoking point. Transfer 6 to 8 murkus at a time to the hot oil and fry to a golden-brown till crisp, turning over twice or thrice. Let the oil heat up again to smoking point between each batch.

Green Gram Murku Makes 12 pieces

INGREDIENTS

Yellow moong dal (husked green gram), steamed or boiled with just enough water till soft 250 g

Rice, washed and aired on a piece of cloth till dry and powder 375 g

Butter 2 tbsp

Cumin 1 tsp

Sesame seeds 1 rounded tsp

Red chilli powder 1 tsp

Salt to taste

Ghee or oil for deep-frying

METHOD

- Grind the cooked dal.
- Add the rest of the ingredients except ghee or oil. Mix and prepare a soft dough using water it necessary. Knead well.
- Press through a murku mould and fry as in Arrowroot Murku (page 140).

Kodabala Murku Makes 8 pieces

INGREDIENTS

Wheat flour 1 loosely-packed cup

Ghee, melted 1 tbsp

Rice flour ¼ cup

Semolina (rava) ¼ cup

Coconut, finely-grated and crushed ¼ cup

Red chilli powder 1 tsp

Cumin 1 tsp

Sesame seeds 1 tsp

Salt to taste

Oil 2 cups

METHOD

- Heat the ghee and roast the wheat flour for a few minutes.
- Mix all the ingredients together. Gradually add enough water to prepare a soft dough.
- Heat the oil.
- Knead the dough well and divide into marble-sized pellets. On a wooden board, using your fingers, roll each pellet into a 6-inch long, ½-inch thick elongated form and shape into two or three concentric circles in the pattern of a murku. Fry like the Arrowroot Murku (page 140).

Sev

Makes 200 g

INGREDIENTS

Besan (gram flour) 250 g

Rice flour 1 rounded tbsp

Green chillies 1

Red chilli powder 1 tsp

Asafoetida (hing) powder ¼ tsp

Butter 1 tbsp

Salt to taste

Oil for deep-frying

METHOD

- Crush salt and chillies in 1 tablespoon of water. Strain, discard skin and seeds.
- Combine all the ingredients except oil and prepare a very soft dough using sufficient quantity of water.
- Press the dough through a sev mould directly into oil kept at smoking point. Reduce the heat to a low flame and fry till crisp, turning over twice or thrice.

Tip: You can use one level teaspoon of omum (ajwain) powder in place of asafoetida powder. Or grind 1 onion, ½-inch long piece of ginger and 1 sprig curry leaves to a smooth paste and use in place of asafoetida powder.

A thicker variety of sev called Karo can be made by adding one more knob of butter to the sev dough and pressing it through a sev mould with bigger perforations.

Savoury Beaten Rice & Cashewnut Mix (Chudva)

Makes 200 g

INGREDIENTS

Thick poha (thick beaten rice) 125 g

Cashewnuts, roughly chopped 75 g

A big pinch of turmeric powder

Table salt to taste

One-fourth of a copra (dried coconut)

SEASONING

Oil ½ tsp

A pinch of mustard seeds

Curry leaves 2 sprigs

Red chilli powder ½ tsp

METHOD

- Heat 2 cups of oil to a smoking point, preferable in a deep-fryer, and fry the poha in 15 batches. The rice sizzles and puffs up immediately. It needs to be lifted out of the hot oil before the colour darkens. Let the oil heat up to smoking point in between each batch.

- Fry the chopped cashewnuts in the same oil till golden brown. Mix with the poha, turmeric and salt.

- Grate or slice the copra. I prefer to do half grated and half sliced. Toast the slices on a non-stick pan first. Remove and toast the grated copra till light brown.

- Heat half a teaspoon of oil, pop the mustard seeds and fry the curry leaves. Take off the heat and add the chilli powder to the oil and immediately pour over the copra.

- Add the poha mix and stir for 10 minutes more. When completely cool, store in an airtight container.

Plantain Pith Pakoras

Makes 16 pieces

INGREDIENTS

Plantain pith (banana stem), finely-chopped ½ cup

Red chilli powder ½ tsp (or green chillies, minced 2)

Onion, finely-chopped 1

Salt to taste

Besan (gram flour) 2 tbsp

Water 1 tbsp

Ghee or oil for deep-frying

Yogurt ½ cup

METHOD

- Steam the plantain pith pieces and drain the water.
- Use a pestle and mortar to mash the chillies, onion and salt together.
- Combine the plantain pith, mashed ingredients, besan and water in a bowl and mix well.
- Heat the oil to smoking point and drop 1½-inch balls of this mixture into the hot oil. Fry them in batches of 6 to 8 till golden brown turning over frequently.
- Mix the yogurt till smooth, add salt if desired and drop the fried pakoras in it. Mix till well coated and serve.

Tip: The pakoras can also be served without yogurt.

Green Pepper Fries (Capsicum Baje)

Makes 48 pieces

INGREDIENTS

Green peppers (capsicum) 4 Spices

A pinch of mustard seeds

Black peppercorns 6

Coriander seeds ½ tsp

A pinch of cumin seeds

A pinch of turmeric powder

A pinch of asafoetida (hing) powder

A tiny pinch of fenugreek seeds

Tamarind ½-inch ball (or tamarind paste ¼ tsp)

Besan (gram flour) 2 tbsp

Butter 1 tsp

Rice flour 1 tbsp

Salt to taste

Oil for deep-frying

METHOD

- Slice the green peppers into 12 pieces in the length.
- Grind the spices into a powder.
- Make a paste using the tamarind with 2 tbsp of water. (Skip this step if you are using paste.)
- Combine the green peppers, spices, tamarind paste, besan and salt in a bowl.
- Heat the oil and fry over medium heat till crisp, turning over often. Serve hot.

Tip: ¾-inch cauliflower florets can be used instead of green peppers.

Breadfruit Bondas

Makes 12 pieces

INGREDIENTS

Breadfruit (small), skinned, steamed and mashed ¼ piece

Coconut, grated 1 tbsp

Onion (small), finely-chopped 1

Green chilli, minced 1

A handful of coriander leaves, chopped

Red chilli powder ¼ tsp (optional)

Salt to taste

Besan (gram flour) 3 tbsp

A pinch of red chilli powder

A big pinch of asafoetida (hing) powder

Salt ¼ tsp

Oil for deep-frying

METHOD

- Crush the coconut, onion, green chilli, coriander leaves, chilli powder (1/4 tsp optional) and salt using a pestle and mortar.
- Make a stiff batter of the besan, pinches of red chilli and asafoetida, and salt by adding water gradually.
- Mix the steamed and mashed breadfruit with the crushed ingredients. Mix well and divide into 12 equal portions. Roll into balls and flatten between the palms into a circle.
- Dip the flat bondas into the batter.
- Heat oil and fry the bondas, four at a time, till golden brown turning over often.

Tip: A mash of 2 medium-sized boiled potatoes and ½ cup steamed cauliflower florets can be substituted for the breadfruit.

Thinglad

Makes 350 g

INGREDIENTS

Arrowroot (ararot) flour 1 cup

Yellow moong dal (husked green gram)
1 cup

Rice flour ¼ cup

Red chilli powder 1 level tsp

Cumin ½ tsp

Salt to taste

Oil for deep-frying

METHOD

- Make a smooth powder of the arrowroot flour. Tie the flour in a piece of thick cloth and steam for 15 minutes.
- Steam or boil the dal in just enough water till tender. Drain the dal and discard water.
- Grind the dal to a smooth paste. Add the rest of the ingredients except cumin and oil. Grind again for a few more minutes.
- Use the dal mixture to make a dough. Add the cumin and knead well. Press the dough through a three-holed murku mould directly into oil kept at smoking point. Reduce the heat and fry over a low flame to a golden brown, turning over twice or thrice.

Colocasia Leaf Rolls with Lentil Filling (Pathravade)

Makes 20

INGREDIENTS

Colocasia leaves (arvi leaves, medium-sized) or cabbage leaves (large) 12

MASALA

Tuvar dal (pigeon pea lentils) or yellow moong dal (husked green gram), soaked in hot water for 30 minutes 75 g

One-fourth of a coconut

Dry red chillies 1-3

A pinch of asafetida (hing) powder

Salt ¼ tsp (or to taste)

METHOD

- Wash and wipe the leaves dry.
- Roast the dry red chillies in a pan till light brown. Grind with the coconut, salt and asafoetida.
- Drain the lentils and add to the mixer. Grind along with the coconut mixture to make a very smooth paste. Divide the paste into 12 equal portions.
- Place one leaf face down, with the stem side facing upwards, on a chopping board. Spread one portion of the masala paste on the top of the leaf. Put another leaf on top of the first and repeat the process. Continue till all the leaves and masala paste is used.
- Fold in the edges of the leaves for about two inches. Roll gently but firmly from the stalk end to the tip into a cylinder. If the cylinder starts unwinding, tie with a string at both ends and in the middle, as well. Cut into quarter-inch thick slices and arrange them on a plate.
- Steam for 45 minutes over a steady heat.

Tip: If you are substituting the arvi leaves with cabbage leaves, add a medium-sized onion to the masala ingredients.

Chutneys &
Chutney Powders

◆◆◆

Green Apple & Mango Ginger Chutney Serves 4

INGREDIENTS

Sour cooking apple, peeled, cored and chopped into small cubes 1

Jaggery or sugar 1 tsp

Butter or ghee 1 tsp

Water 50 ml

Salt to taste

MASALA

Green chillies 1-3

A clove of garlic

Mango ginger ½-inch piece

Tamarind ¼-inch ball
(or a pinch of tamarind paste)

Coconut, grated 1 tbsp

A pinch of turmeric powder

A pinch of asafoetida (hing) powder

Mustard seeds 1 tsp

Water 50 ml

METHOD

- Cook the apple with sugar, salt, butter and water over low heat till tender. Cool.
- Grind the masala ingredients in a blender to make a smooth paste.
- Mix the masala with the cooked apple and stir well. Serve with dosa, idli or parathas.

Dosa Chutney Serves 4

INGREDIENTS

One-fourth of a coconut, cut into bits

Curry leaves 1 sprig

Green chillies 1-3

Onion, cut 1 tsp

Fresh ginger, minced ½ tsp

A handful of fresh green coriander

Water, boiled 3 tbsp

Salt to taste

SEASONING

Oil 1 tsp

A pinch of mustard seeds

Lime juice ½ tsp (or yogurt 12 tsp)

METHOD

- Grind the coconut, curry leaves, chillies, onion and ginger into a paste along with the water and salt.
- Heat the oil and fry the mustard seeds. Pour over the paste and mix well.
- Add the lime juice or yogurt and mix again. Serve with dosas or idlis.

Teasel Gourd Chutney (Phagil Chutney)

Makes about 50 g

INGREDIENTS

Teasel gourds (kantola/kakora) 2

Salt ½ tsp

Vegetable oil 2 tbsp

One-fourth of a coconut

Green chillies 1-3

Tamarind ½-inch ball

Cumin ½ tsp

Salt to taste

METHOD

- Top and tail the gourds. Cut them into small pieces. Add the salt, mix well and let it stand for 15 minutes. Then squeeze the gourd pieces and discard the juice.

- Heat the oil and fry the cumin. Remove the cumin seeds from the pan and fry the gourd in the same oil over low heat till brown.

- Grind the fried gourd with coconut, chillies and tamarind along with the fried cumin seeds and salt to make a smooth chutney.

Tip: Kakora, or kantola, has a nice nutty flavour and this chutney makes a delicious accompaniment to rice dosai or chapatis.

You can also make this recipe by substituting the teasel gourd with 2 small bitter gourds (karela). When doing so, use 2 cloves of garlic and a pinch of asafoetida (hing) instead of cumin.

Potato Chutney (Batat Gozzu)

Serves 2

INGREDIENTS

Potatoes (medium-sized) 2

Green chillies (small) 2

Water, boiled 1 cup

Coconut, grated 2 tsp (optional)

Yogurt (curd) 1 tbsp

Salt to taste

SEASONING

Vegetable oil 2 tsp

A pinch of mustard seeds

Curry leaves 1 sprig

Dry red chilli (small) 1

A big pinch of asafoetida (hing) powder

Coriander leaves, chopped 1 tbsp (optional)

METHOD

- Boil, peel and mash the potatoes.
- Crush the green chillies with the water and discard the skins.
- Mix the potato, chilli water, coconut, curd and salt.
- In a small pan, heat the oil and pop the mustard seeds. Fry the red chilli, take the pan off the heat and add the asafoetida. Swirl around and pour over the mashed potato.

Tip: Use a teaspoon of tamarind paste or juice of a lime in place of the curd. You can also use a cooked and mashed tomato, bilimbi or green mango.

A simple Konkani favourite that goes well with Dalithoi and rice

Bilimbi Chutney

Serves 4

INGREDIENTS

Bilimbis (bimbla fruit) 175 g

Sugar 60 g

Vinegar ¼ cup

Salt ¼ tsp

Dates, stoned 15 g

Garlic cloves, peeled 5

Ginger, peeled 15 g

Raisins 25 g

Water 2 tbsp

A pinch of clove powder

A pinch of mace powder

A pinch of nutmeg

A pinch of cinnamon powder

A big pinch of pepper powder

METHOD

- Slice the bilimbis into ¼-inch thick discs.
- Add the sugar, vinegar and salt, mix well and set aside.
- Grind the dates, garlic, ginger and raisins into a rough paste with the water.
- Combine this paste with the fruit and cook over low heat, stirring constantly till it reaches a jam-like consistency.
- Mix the powdered spices and add to the fruit mixture. Continue to cook for another 5 minutes. Remove from heat, cool and bottle.

Tip: Bilimbi is a sour fruit, generally eaten raw with salt and chilli in the Konkan area.

Made from fruits of the 'cucumber' tree, this is a delicious sweet sour chutney.

Coriander Leaf Chutney Serves 4

INGREDIENTS

Coriander leaves 1 cup

Coconut, grated 2 tbsp

Green chillies 2-4 (according to taste)

Tamarind ½-inch ball (or tamarind paste ¼ tsp)

Salt to taste

METHOD

- Wash the coriander and spread out on a tea towel to dry.
- Grind the coconut, chillies and tamarind to a smooth paste in a mixer.
- Add the coriander leaves and salt and continue grinding till absolutely smooth.

Tip: Use only the leaves and tender stalks of green coriander. Do not add water. Can be used as a sandwich spread as well.

Mango Chutney Serves 4

INGREDIENTS

Green mangoes (kairee) 2

One-fourth of a coconut, grated

Garlic cloves 4

A pinch of turmeric

Red chilli powder ⅓ tsp (or 2 green chillies)

SEASONING

Oil 2 tsp

A pinch of mustard seeds

A big pinch of asafoetida (hing) powder

METHOD

- Boil the green mangoes till soft. Peel and remove the flesh.
- Grind the mangoes with the grated coconut, garlic, turmeric and chillies.
- In a small pan, heat the oil and fry the mustard seeds till they pop. Remove from heat and add the asafoetida, giving it a stir and then pouring it over the mango mixture. Cool, then serve with rice or parathas.

Indian Pennywort Chutney (Gotu Kola Chutney)

Serves 4

INGREDIENTS

Indian pennywort (brahmi) with 30 leaves (with stalks)

Coconut, grated 2 tbsp

Green chillies 2

Tamarind ½-inch ball or (or a pinch of tamarind paste)

Ginger, minced ¼ tsp

Salt to taste

METHOD

- Wash the brahmi leaves and dry on a clean tea towel.

- Grind the leaves into a smooth paste with the coconut, chillies, tamarind, ginger and salt in a blender.

Tip: Brahmi, also known as ekpani, is a medicinal plant used in Ayurvedic medicine. It is eaten in some form almost every day in the Konkan region and in Sri Lanka. This chutney can is a tasty and healthy sandwich spread.

Curry Leaf Chutney Powder (Karbeva Chutney)

Serves 4

INGREDIENTS

Fresh curry leaves (kadipatta) 10 sprigs
(or ½ lightly packed cup)

Half a coconut, finely-grated

Chana dal (husked Bengal gram) ¼ cup

Dry red chillies 5-8

Tamarind paste ¼ tsp

Salt ½ tsp

METHOD

- Dry roast the curry leaves and grated coconut together in a frying pan, till leaves are crisp and coconut is light brown in colour. Remove the curry leaves from the coconut and set aside. Do not roast the curry leaves separately as they get charred.

- Roast the red chillies next.

- Remove the chillies from the pan and then roast the dal over a low fire till pale brown. Do not hurry this process as the dal burns easily.

- Grind the curry leaves and dal in a coffee grinder till the mixture resembles fine breadcrumbs or semolina (rava).

- Next, grind the coconut, tamarind and salt together.

- Mix both powders together and keep in a clean dry jar. Serve with rice and curd, idli and dosa.

Tip: You can substitute the curry leaves in the recipe with 50 g of fresh green coriander, 2 pods of garlic or 1/2 cup roasted peanuts.

Lentil Chutney Powder (Parpu Podi)

Serves 4

INGREDIENTS

Chana dal (husked Bengal gram) 60 g

Yellow moong dal (husked green gram) 60 g

Urad dal (husked black gram) 30 g

Tuvar dal (split pigeon peas) 60 g

Dry red chillies 15

Fenugreek seeds 1 level tsp

Cumin seeds 2 tsp

Black peppercorns 1 heaped tsp

Two pieces of fresh turmeric, each 1½-inch long (or turmeric powder) ¾ tsp

A pea-sized piece of asafoetida

Salt 2 tsp

METHOD

- Dry roast the curry leaves and grated coconut together in a frying pan, till leaves Dry roast each lentil and spice separately in a frying pan over a low fire till light brown.
- Grind together into a medium-fine powder, then stir well to mix and store in a clean dry jar. Serve with rice and clarified butter/*ghee*.

Tip: Strictly speaking, this is a recipe from Andhra Pradesh but is popular with all south Indians including the Konkani community. A tablespoon of this powder makes a tasty accompaniment to idlis and dosas:

As a variation, roast 11 cloves and a 4-inch cinnamon stick and powder along with the above ingredients.

Pickles

Wood Apple Pickle

Makes 1 cup

INGREDIENTS

Sour wood apples (kavath) 2

Water ½ cup

Jaggery 1 tsp

SEASONING

Oil 3 tbsp

Green chillies, minced 4-10

A small pod of garlic (16 cloves), peeled and crushed

Mild asafoetida (hing) powder 3 tsp

ROAST SEPARATELY

Mustard seeds 2 heaped tsp

Black peppercorn 1 tsp

Fenugreek seeds ½ tsp

Sesame seeds 2 tbsp (do not brown)

Sea salt 1 heaped tsp

METHOD

- Scoop the pulp out of the wood apples. You should get about 2 cups of pulp.
- Mix the wood apple pulp with the water and strain to remove seeds and threads.
- Add the jaggery to the strained pulp.
- Using a pestle and mortar, grind the green chillies and garlic together.
- Heat the oil and fry the chillies and garlic. Take off heat and add the asafoetida to the oil.
- Pour this seasoning over the wood apple paste. Cook together over a low flame till reduced by half to about 1 cup. Remove from heat.
- Powder all the roasted spices, sesame seeds and salt, and mix with the wood apple mixture. When it cools fill into a clean jar. Keeps for up to a week when refrigerated.

Tip: To test for ripeness, drop the wood apple on the ground from a 4-feet height. If it bounces, it is unripe. If it falls like a stone it is ready to use. To ripen wood apples quickly, place them in a sack of rice. They will be ready to use in 2 to 3 days.

This chutney tastes best with idlis, dosas, rice or parathas.

Green Chilli Pickle Makes 75 g

INGREDIENTS

Green chillies 100 g

Lime juice 75 ml

Juice from grated fresh ginger 2 tbsp

Salt 2 tbsp

Toddy vinegar 2 tbsp

Sesame seeds, roasted and powdered 2 tbsp

Oil 1 tbsp

A pinch of mustard seeds

Mild asafoetida (hing) powder ½ tsp

Turmeric powder ¼ tsp

METHOD

- Wash the green chillies and add them to 6 cups of boiling water. Stir and immediately drain all the water. Spread them out on a clean tea towel to dry. Cut off the stalks and make a ¼-inch slit from the top end.
- Add the sesame seed powder to the chillies and mix well.
- In a small pan, heat the oil and fry the mustard seeds till they pop. Remove from heat, add the turmeric and asafoetida and pour this seasoning over the green chillies. Stir well. This can be stored in a clean dry jar for 2 months before using.

Bilimbi Pickle Makes 250 g

INGREDIENTS

Bilimbi (bimbla fruit), small to medium-sized 18 pieces

Green chillies, sliced 3-6

Garlic cloves, sliced 9

Vinegar 2 tbsp

Mild asafoetida (hing) powder ¼ tsp

Salt 2 tbsp

Water, boiled 50 ml

METHOD

- Slice the bilimbi breadth-wise, into circles.
- Place all the ingredients in a clean pickling jar, and shake well to ensure the fruit is coated with salt. Wrap the lid of the jar with paper and tie with a string. Keep in the sun daily for 7 days.

Mango Ginger Pickle (Aamhaldi Pickle)

Makes 100 g

INGREDIENTS

Mango ginger (ambra), washed, peeled and chopped 125 g

Garlic, peeled ½ pod

Salt 2 heaped tsp

Green chillies, chopped 1-5

Sesame oil 2 tbsp

Mild asafoetida (hing) powder 2 tsp

Black peppercorns 2 tsp

Mustard seeds 1 tsp

Fenugreek seeds ¼ tsp

Tamarind 1½-inch ball soaked in ½ cup of water

METHOD

- Crush the mango ginger and garlic with a pestle and mortar. Add salt and keep pounding.
- Heat the oil and fry the chillies till light brown. Remove from heat and add the asafoetida powder.
- Combine the crushed mango ginger and the chilli seasoning. Add the powdered spices and tamarind juice. Mix thoroughly and store in a clean jar. Consume within 5 days.

Prawn Pickle

Makes 500 g

INGREDIENTS

Shelled prawns, cut into 1-inch pieces 500 g

Vegetable oil 125 g

MASALA

A pinch of omum (ajwain) powder

A big pinch of cumin powder

A big pinch of fenugreek, powdered

Garam masala powder (page 23) 3 tsp

Red chilli powder 3 tsp

Turmeric powder ½ tsp

GREEN MASALA

Large onions, sliced 3

Green chillies, sliced 7

Garlic cloves, sliced 12

Salt to taste

Juice of 2 small limes

Vinegar 50 ml

METHOD

- Combine all the spices.
- Mix the onions, chillies, garlic and salt.
- Boil the lime juice and mix with the vinegar.
- In a pan, heat the oil to smoking point and add the mixed masala powder. Give it a stir and add the prawns. Stir again and add the green masala and salt. Cook till onions turn brown. Remove from heat and allow to cool.
- Pour in the boiled lime juice and vinegar. Bring to a boil again simmer for 3 minutes and remove from heat. Cool and bottle in clean dry jar. Consume within a week.

Star Fruit Pickle (Karmbal Mixture)

Makes 250 g

INGREDIENTS

Star fruits (kamrakh) 25 pieces

Green chillies 20

Salt to taste

Mustard seeds 1 tbsp

Black peppercorns 1 tsp

Dry red chillies 20

Garlic pods 4

1½-inch ginger pieces 4

Water 1½ cups

Oil 2 tbsp

Juice of 4 limes

Limes, sliced in circles 2

METHOD

- Wash the star fruit. Remove the ribs. Slice into ¼-inch thick discs.
- Slit 12 of the green chillies in half and add along with the salt to the star fruit. Cover and keep aside for 3 days stirring once daily.
- Roast the mustard seeds and peppercorns separately. Powder together.
- Grind the red chillies, garlic and ginger with the water in a paste.
- Heat oil to smoking point. Fry the remaining 12 chillies in this oil and stir for a while. Add the powdered spices and the red chilli paste. Stir once and remove from heat. Allow it to cool.
- Add the star fruit mixture and lime juice to the chilli paste.
- Add the lime slices. Stir well to mix and fill in a clean dry pickle jar. Stir once or twice daily for three days before using.

Fresh Kohl Rabi Pickle (Knol Kol Pickle)

Makes 50 g

INGREDIENTS

Half a kohl rabi (knol kol), sliced and cut into ¼-inch pieces

Salt 1 tsp

Green mango (kairee), chopped 1 tbsp

Oil 1 tsp

Salt to taste

Coconut, grated and roasted till brown 2 tbsp

Dry red chilli 1

Mustard seeds ¼ tsp

A big pinch of turmeric powder

A big pinch of asafoetida (hing) powder

Water ⅓ cup

METHOD

- Sprinkle the salt over the chopped knol kol and let it stand for 10 minutes. Squeeze the excess water from the knol kol.
- Add the chopped mango pieces, oil and salt (if required).
- Mix the roasted coconut, red chilli, mustard seeds, turmeric and asafoetida and grind in a mixer till smooth and fine. Add the water and make into a paste.
- Coat the knol kol and mango pieces with the paste, stir well and serve as an accompaniment to any meal. This pickle stays for a week when refrigerated.

Desserts

Arrowroot & Cardamom Slices (Duddali)

Makes 12 pieces

INGREDIENTS

Arrowroot (ararot) ¼ cup

Water ¾ cup

Milk ¾ cup

Cardamom, skinned and powdered 6

Sugar ¼ cup

METHOD

- Mix the arrowroot with 8-10 cups of water and let it stand for 2-3 hours. Decant and discard the clear water on top.
- To the settled flour add the water, milk, cardamom and sugar, mixing well. Cook over low heat, stirring briskly, till the mixture takes on a bluish tinge. Remove from heat.
- Grease a flat tin, pan or plate and transfer the cooked arrowroot mixture to it. Flatten with spatula or fingers to ½-inch thickness. When cool cut into squares or diamonds.

Papaya Halwa

Makes 28 pieces

INGREDIENTS

Papaya, skinned and cut into cubes 750 g

Milk 1¼ cups

Orange juice (or tomato juice) 1 cup

Sugar 1 cup (add up to ½ cup more to taste)

Ghee ⅓ cup

Cardamom powder ⅓ tsp

METHOD

- Cook the chopped papaya in milk till soft, about 12 minutes. Don't worry if the milk curdles. Mash or blend into a paste and pour into a wide heavy-bottomed pan.
- Add the juice and sugar to the paste and cook, stirring frequently till the mixture boils down to about one-third the original amount and becomes semi-solid. When boiling, the mixture will spit so be careful when stirring.
- Pour in the melted ghee, reduce the heat and keep stirring till the mixture leaves the sides of the pan. It will become a large ball that moves together when stirred.
- Transfer a teaspoon of the mixture on to a plate, allow it to cool and then test for readiness by pressing it between your thumb and finger. If the mixture does not stick to your fingers, the halwa is ready. This makes about a cup-and-a-half of halwa.
- Remove the halwa from heat, add the cardamom powder and mix well.
- Line a plate with butter paper and press the mixture down with a spatula till it's half-thickened, even and firm. This makes a circle of about 7-inch diameter. When cool, cut into squares or diamonds.

Tip: Choose a papaya which is well seasoned and yellowish but not fully ripe.

Sweet Gram Khichadi (Gram Payasam/Mudganey)

Serves 4

INGREDIENTS

Chana dal (husked Bengal Gram) 1 cup

Water 2 cups

Cashewnuts, chopped ½ cup

Jaggery, powdered 1 cup

Cardamom, skinned and powdered 8

Rice flour 1 tbsp

Coconut 1

Raisins 1 tbsp

METHOD

- Wash the dal. Bring two cups of water to a boil and add the washed dal to it. Reduce to a simmer and cook till soft.

- Cook the cashewnuts in half-a-cup of water till soft.

- Make 1½ cups coconut milk from the fresh coconut (page 18).

- Combine the cardamom and jaggery.

- Mix the rice flour and 1 cup of thin coconut milk. Cook over low flame for 8 minutes stirring continuously till smooth.

- Add the boiled dal, cashewnuts, cardamom and jaggery mix and bring to a boil. Remove from heat and add the ½ cup of thick coconut milk. Mix well and garnish with raisins. Serve.

Sweet Potato Khichdi (Kanang Khichdi) Serves 6-8

INGREDIENTS

Sweet potato, finely-chopped 12 tbsp

Water 4 tbsp

Coconut, grated 12 tbsp

Ghee 4 tbsp

Raisins 2 tbsp

Cardamom powder ½ tsp

Sugar 4 tbsp

METHOD

- Fry the grated coconut in ghee over a low heat till light brown.
- Add the sweet potato pieces and water to the coconut. Stir, cover and cook over low heat till soft.
- Add the raisins, cardamom powder and sugar and cook, stirring constantly till the mixture becomes a bit sticky and all the syrup is absorbed. Remove from heat and serve hot with dosas or puris.

Tip: Serve in small quantities like a jam, condiment or chutney.

Banana Dumplings (Plantain Modak) Serves 12

INGREDIENTS

Ripe Malabar bananas 2

Rice flour 125 g

A pinch of salt

Cardamom powder ¼ tsp

A big pinch of baking soda

Sugar 1-2 tsp (optional)

Oil or ghee for frying

METHOD

- In a bowl, mash the bananas and add rice flour, salt, cardamom powder, baking soda and sugar together. Mix well to make a smooth dough.
- Heat the oil to smoking point, reduce heat and drop in six 1-inch scoops of dough at a time. Fry till golden brown, stirring often. Bring the oil back to smoking point before dropping in the next batch. Serve hot.

Sweet Gram-filled Flat Bread (Puranpoli/ Ubbati)

Makes 20

INGREDIENTS

FILLING

Chana dal (Husked Bengal Gram) ¾ cup

Sugar or jaggery ¾ cup

Cardamom, skinned and powdered 12

FOR THE DOUGH

Flour 1 cup

Powdered sugar 1 tsp

A big pinch of saffron, soaked in 1 tsp water and mashed

Ghee 1 tbsp

Ghee (for rolling) 4 tbsp

METHOD

- Bring 2 cups of water to the boil and add the washed dal. Cook till tender.

- Drain the water, if any, from the cooked dal. Add sugar and cook over a medium heat, stirring constantly till the mixture becomes quite thick and sticky.

- Remove from the heat and grind to a smooth paste in a blender with the cardamom powder. Do not add any water. Divide into 20 portions.

- Mix the flour, powdered sugar, saffron, 1 tbsp ghee and just enough water to make a soft dough. Knead well for 10 minutes.

- Smear the palm of your left hand with a little ghee and flatten one portion of the dough into a circle 2-inch in diameter.

- Place one portion of the filling in the centre and gather the edges of the dough circle, enclosing the filling while pinching the seams together. Dust with flour.

- Sprinkle some flour over a 9-inch square piece of greaseproof paper and roll the dough ball into a circle about 1/8-inch thick.

- Heat a non-stick frying pan over medium heat, reduce to low when hot and transfer the rolled dough onto the surface. Roast the puranpoli till you see brown spots on the underside. Turn over once or twice till cooked. Wipe the pan in between roasting each poli.

- Brush the polis with some ghee and stack them.

Tip: Store in an airtight container to retain their softness. Keeps for 3-4 days. Heat and serve with ghee.

Coconut & Cashew Sweet Mix (Kanya Hindri)

Serves 4

INGREDIENTS

Coconut 1

Jaggery 125 g

Water 1 cup

Beaten rice (poha) 75 g

Cashewnuts 50 g

Cardamom, skinned and powdered 8

METHOD

- Chop the coconut and dry grind in a mixer.

- Roast the beaten rice till crisp. Powder.

- Fry the cashewnut in a little oil till golden brown. (It can also be grated before adding.)

- Dissolve the jaggery in water over medium heat to make a syrup. When the syrup can be drawn into long strings it is ready. Test by dropping a bit of syrup into cold water. If the drop can be rolled into a sticky ball, it's done.

- Add the coarsely-ground coconut till it absorbs the syrup and appears dry to the touch.

- Swiftly add the powdered beaten rice, cashewnuts and cardamom. Stir well. Divide into small greased containers and serve when cool.

Panchakajjai

Serves 4

INGREDIENTS

Chana dal (husked Bengal gram) 3 tbsp

Half a large coconut

Sugar 3 heaped tbsp

Cardamom, skinned and powdered 9

Sesame seeds (til) 1 tbsp

METHOD

- Roast the dal over low heat till brown. Grind in a coffee grinder till it acquires the consistency of semolina (rava).
- Grate the coconut and crush together with the sugar and cardamom.
- Roast the sesame seeds over a low flame till light brown.
- Add the coconut mixture and sesame seeds to the ground dal. Mix well and serve with ghee.

Tip: Use roasted yellow moong dal (husked green gram) instead of the Bengal gram or beaten rice.

Peanut or Cashewnut Brittle (Nelkadle Chikki)

Makes 12 pieces

INGREDIENTS

Peanuts, roasted and skinned, roughly broken 1 cup

Jaggery ¾ cup

A pinch of cardamom

Water 2 tbsp

METHOD

- Heat the jaggery with the water. When the jaggery melts and begins to boil, add the cardamom powder and mix. Keep cooking till it becomes a thick syrup. Test for readiness by pouring a drop or two in ice cold water. If it hardens, the jaggery is ready. Swiftly add the peanuts and stir well.

- Remove immediately on to a greased pan and spread with a spatula. (It will be too hot to touch.)

- Score the surface into squares with a knife. Break into pieces when cool.

Tip: You can use cashewnuts instead of peanuts.

Whole Wheat Appe

Makes 25 pieces

INGREDIENTS

Whole wheat flour ¾ cup

Milk ½ cup

Coconut, grated 3 tbsp

Sugar 3 tbsp

Cardamom, skinned and powdered 9

A pinch of salt

Water 3 tbsp

Ghee for frying

METHOD

- Grind all the ingredients together into a paste in a mixer, adding the water to make it smooth.
- Heat an appe patra (or appam patra, very similar to a Dutch poffertjes pan) over medium heat. Pour a teaspoon of ghee into each depression and heat to smoking point.
- Drop a teaspoon of the batter into each mould and fry till light brown turning over twice or thrice with a fork.

Glossary

◆◆◆

ENGLISH	HINDI	KANNADA	KONKANI	MARATHI
Mango Ginger	Aamhaldi	Marasunti	Aamhaldi	Ambehalad
Omum	Ajwain	Oma	Onvo	Ova
Almond	Badam	Badam	badamb	Badam
Gooseberry	Amla	Nellikai	Avalo	Avla
Apple	Seb	Sebinahannu	Saparjal	Sapharchand
Apricot	Jardaloo	Jaral	Jardal	Jardaloo
Arrowroot	Araru, Ararot	Kuvehittu	Kuvyapeeth	..
Colocasia	Arvi	Kesuvinagadde	Alvamande	Alu
Asafoetida	Hing	Hingu	Hingu	Hing
Ash-gourd	Petha	Boodakumbalakai	Kuvale	Kohla
Wheat flour	Atta	Godhi hittu	Peeth	Peeth
Banana	Kela	Balekai	Kele	Kela
Bay Leaves	Tejpatha	..	..	
Beaten Rice	Poha	Avalakki	Phovu	Phove
Beetroot	Chugander	Gaajinagadde	Beetroot	Beet
Bengal Gram	Chana dal	Kadale bela	Chano	Chane
Bengal Gram flour	Besan	Kadalehittu	Chanapeeth	Besan
Okra	Bhindi	Bendekai	Bhend	Bhendi
Bilimbi	Bimbli fruit	Bilimbi	Bimbul	Bimbul
Bitter Gourd	Karela	Hagalakai	Karathe	Karla
Black Gram	Urad	Uddina bele	Udidu	Udidh
Bottle Gourd	Lauki	Soraikai	Gharduddi	Duddi-bhopla
Bread	Double roti	Nanurotti	Bread	Pav
Breadfruit	…	Divigujje	Divikadgi (Jivkadgi)	…
Aubergine	Baigan	Badanekai	Vaingan	Vaangi
Butter	Makkhan	Benne	Loni	Loni
Buttermilk	Chaach	Majjige	Thaak	Thaak
Cabbage	Patta Gobi	Kossugadde	Cabbage	Kobi
Capsicum	Shimla mirch	Dodda Menasenakai	Donnemirsang	Bhoplamirchi
Cardamom	Elaichi	Elakki	Yelu	Belchei
Carrot	Gajar	Carrot	Carrot	Gajar
Cashewnut	Kaju	Gerubeeja	Kazzubi	Kaju

ENGLISH	HINDI	KANNADA	KONKANI	MARATHI
Cauliflower	Phoolgobi	Cauliflower	Cauliflower	Phulkobi
Chillies-red	Lalmirch	Onamenasu	Sukkimirsang	Lal mirchi
Chillies-green	Harimirch	Hasimenasu	Tharnimirsang	Hirve mirchi
Cinnamon	Dalchini	Dalchini	Dalchini	Dalchini
Cloves	Laung	Lavang	Lavang	Lavang
Cluster Beans	Govarphalli	Chavalikai	Mitkesaang	Govarchishenga
Coconut	Nariyal	Thenginakai	Narlu	Naral
Dried coconut	Copra	Kobbare	Khobre	Sukakhopra
Coriander	Dhania	Kothambari	Kothambari	Dhania
Cream	Malai	Halinakene	Sayi	Saya
Cucumber	Kheera	Southekai	Magge	Kakdi
Curd	Dahi	Mosaru	Dhal	Dhai
Curry Leaves	Kadipatta	Karibevu	Karbevu	Kadhilimb
Dates	Khazoor	Khazoor	Khazzuru	Khazoor
Dal	Dal	Bele	Daali	Dal
Milk	Doodh	Haalu	Doodh	Doodh
Drumstick		Nuggekodu	Mashingasaang	Shevagiyachashenga
Egg	Anda	Motte	Thanthe	Anda
Indian pennywort	Brahmi Leaves / Ekpani	Ondelega	Ekpani	..
Fish	Machi	Meenu	Jhalke	Maase
French beans	Beans	..	..	Pharasbi
Garlic	Lasun	Bellulli	Losun	Lasun
Clarified Butter	Ghee	Thuppa	Thoop	Thoop
Gherkins	Kundru	Thondekai	Thendle	Tondali
Ginger	Adrak	Shunti	Alle	Alla
Grapes	Angoor	Drakshihannu	Darksha	Draksha
Green-gram	Moong	Hesaru bele	Moogu	Moong
Horse-gram	Kulthi	Huruli	Kulithu	Kulthi
Jackfruit	Katial	Halasinahannu	Phanas	Phanas
Jaggery	Gur	Bella	God	Gool
Nutmeg	Jaiphal	Jajikai	Jaiphal	Jaiphal
Sorghum	Jawar	Akkijoin	Saamijolu	Jawari
Cumin	Jeera	Jeerige	Jeera	Jeera
Star Fruit	Kamrakh	Dharehuli	Karmbal	..
Saffron	Zaffran	Kesari	Keshar	Keshar
Milk Solids	Thickened milk	Khova	Khavo	Khava
Poppy seeds	Khus Khus	Ghasa ghase	Khus khus	Khus khus
Kohl Rabi	Ganthgobi	Knol kol	Knol kol	Knol kol
Wild potato	..	Sambrabugadde	Kook	..

ENGLISH	HINDI	KANNADA	KONKANI	MARATHI
Lime	Nimbu	Limbehannu	Limbiyo	Limbu
Mace	Javanthri	Pathri	Pathri	Jaipathri
White flour	Maida	Maida	Maida	Maida
Mango	Aam	Mavinahannu	Aambo	Aamba
Red lentils	Lal masoor	Mysore bele	Masuri	Masoor
Peas	Matar	Batani	Batano	Vatane
Chayote	Chow Chow	Seemebadanekai	..	..
Fenugreek leaves	Methi	Menthe	Metthi	Methi
Mint	Pudina	..	..	Pudina
Mustard	Rai	Sasive	Saasam	Mohri
Mutton	Maas	Mamsa	Maas	Mams
Onion	Pyaz	Neerulli	Piyayu	Kanda
Orange	Santhra	Kithalehannu	Sonnaringa	Santhra
Spinach	Palak	Palak soppu	Palak	Palak
Papaya	Papita	Papaya	Popashphal	Poppaya
Pea dal	Putani	Putani	Batabedaali	Vatanyachidhal
Black pepper	Kali mirch	Kalumenasu	Meere	Meeri
Teasel Gourd	Kantola	Adavihagalakai	Phagil	Kantooli
Pineapple	Ananas	Ananas	Avnaas	Ananas
Plantain	Kela	Balehannu	Kele	Kela
Plantain flower	Kela ka phool	Balehuvu	Bondi	Kelphul
Plantain pith	Kela ka guda	Balendandu	Gabbo	Kaal
Pomegranate	Anar	Dalimbehannu	Dalimb	Dalimba
Potato	Aloo	Batate	Batat	Batata
Prawns	Jhinga	Sigadi (Yetti)	Sungat	Kolambi
Puffed rice	Murmura	Huriakki	Charmburo	Kurmura
Pumpkin	Kaddu	Kumbalakai	Duddi	Thambdabhopla
Radish	Muli	Mullangi	Mullangi	Mula
Raisins	Kishmish	Drakshi	Draksh	Bedana
Semolina	Suji, Rawa	Sajjige	Rulanvu	Rava
Rice	Chaawal	Akki	Thaandul	Thandul
Ridge gourd	Turai	Heerekai	Gosaale	Shirali
Rind	Chilka	Sippe	Saali	Saal
Rose water	Gulab jal	Panneeru	Gulaabaaudak	..
Sago	Sabudana	Sabakki	Saguthaabdul	Sabudana
Salt	Namak	Uppu	Meet	Meet
Snake Gourd	Padwal	Paduvalakai	Poddaale	Padval
Fennel Seeds	Sonf	Shep	Sevi	Badishepa
Elephant Yam	Suran	Sooranagadde	Soornu	Sooran

ENGLISH	HINDI	KANNADA	KONKANI	MARATHI
Spinach, Malabar	Palak	Basale	Vaali	Mayalu
Star Gooseberry	..	Kirinellikai	Razavalo	Razavala
Sugar	Cheeni	Sakkare	Sakkar	Sakhar
Sugar Candy	Misri	Kallusakkare	Khadesakkar	Khadesakhar
Sweet Potato	Rataloo	Genasu	Kanang	Rathal
Tamarind	Imli	Hunasehannu	Chinchamb	Chinch
Tender Bamboo shoots	Banska Ankur	Kanile	Keerlu	..
Tender Cashewnuts	Hara kaju	Yelegerubeeja	Bibbo	Kaju
Szechaun pepper		..	Theppal	Thriphal
Sesame seeds	Til	Ellu	Theelu	Thil
Garden Greens	Garden greens	Harivesoppu	Bhajji	Maat
Pigeon Pea Dal	Tuvar Dal/Arhar	Thogari bele	Thori	Tur
Tomato	Tamatar	Tomato	Tomato	Tomato
Turmeric	Haldi	Hari shina	Haldi	Halad
Vinegar	Seerka	..	..	..
Walnut	Akroot	Akroot	Akjroot	Akroot
Wood Apple	Kat Bel/Kavath	Belphal	Bhelphal	Bhelphal

Acknowledgements

◆◆◆

Many people had a hand in helping get this book out again. I owe thanks to all of them – to my family for unhesitatingly eating my many iffy productions, to my daughter Namita for her support in all aspects of this endeavour, to my friends Neelam Sawani and Mahindra Sinh for encouragement and tutelage, and to Ahalya and Uma Ranganathan, who continue to invite me to their wonderful Konkani table.

About the Author

♦♦♦

Jyotsna Shahane is a filmmaker with a passion for Indian food. In 2004 she started her blog, The Cooks's Cottage, one of a handful of bloggers writing on the subject of local Indian food and recipes at the time. She was named one of the world's favourite food bloggers by *Saveur*, the gourmet food magazine. Jyotsna lives with her husband in Pune.